$PEND YOUR WAY TO WEALTH

Mike Schiano

ALLWORTH PRESS
NEW YORK

Dedication

For my Mother,
the greatest example of unselfish caring, unconditional love,
and unlimited forgiveness anyone could ever have. Through you, God
gave me all of my gifts. You taught three sons how to work hard,
to be survivors during tough times, and to fully enjoy the good things
in life. I can only thank you a million times for all that you have
done for me in my life and continue to do.

I love you, Mom.

Table of Contents

Acknowledgements

I could not have completed this book without the help of several very important people. First and foremost, I want to thank my wife, Lori, for her support of everything I do. As a wife, completely devoted mother, and my best friend, your patience and understanding have been limitless and invaluable. I would not have started, nor ever completed, this book without you believing in me. I love you with all of my heart.

I continue to be inspired and draw a great deal of energy and creativity from my children. Drew, for your help with research, your sincere interest in what I do, and your support. You continue to impress me with your style and your talent. You are going to be a positive inspiration to many people in your life. Brice, for surprising me every day with your creativity, and for making life so colorful. And, Amanda Grace, your smile simply lights up my heart.

I want to thank my grandfather, who passed away in July of 2002 as I was completing the book. He showed me that hard work and attention to detail are the true keys to success.

Thanks to my Aunt Emma for your prayers, laughs, and "do it" attitude.

My special thanks to Tad Crawford, Publisher and President of Allworth Press, for believing in this project and in my abilities. I am grateful to the members of the Allworth Press team, who I have had the great honor of working with, especially: Nicole Potter, Jessica Rozler, Michael Madole, and Birte Pampel. Thank you for making me feel so welcome and comfortable. Your passion for what you do is contagious.

For her tireless work on behalf of our radio show, e-zine, and Web site, I want to thank Anna Cohen.

Introduction

"If we command our wealth, we shall be rich and free. If our wealth commands us, we are poor indeed."
—Edmund Burke

It is with great pleasure that I present these words to you, and I sincerely hope they will inspire and incite you to take action that will greatly improve the total quality of your life, and that of your family.

This book will give you specific information and strategies that you can use immediately to begin to make better financial decisions. The power and financial leverage you gain from managing your money properly is enormous. In our market system, spending large amounts of money is required in order to survive; my goal is to turn you into an empowered, confident consumer.

I do not treat spending like a disease. Let's face it; there is no way to avoid spending money in the real world. You can't turn on a light in your home without spending money. Rather than attempt to "cure" your spending, I celebrate it. Spending money, in my opinion, is not only a necessity; it is the favorite pastime for Americans. Most people love to spend money. Look at the numbers. In March 2002, revolving credit—mostly credit card debt—reached $704.7 billion. Consumer spending rose in the same month to $7.29 trillion. This is happening in the middle of a badly performing economy with many job losses.

One reason that consumers have increased their spending is that, despite the recession, incomes continue to rise, and as one of my mentors used to say, "There is no income you cannot outspend."

I have called upon my years of working with those who want to learn how to manage their money better, get out of debt, and build a richer lifestyle, to present a down-to-earth, fresh approach to the subject of successful personal money management.

Spend Your Way to Wealth will give you advice and practical steps toward using our free-market system to your advantage. This book refutes the advice of many popular financial gurus who urge you to do without the things you want for the next forty years with the hope you will have enough money saved to enjoy the last few years of your life.

Spend Your Way To Wealth is an action plan that will give you powerful strategies to achieve a higher quality of life, not in forty years, but, virtually, right away. And you can have this richer lifestyle without sacrifice, without driving old cars, without living in small houses, and without telling your kids no all of the time. I suggest that you can have everything you want in life, and actually enjoy life now, without guilt, if you are smart about how you spend.

Those who tell you to stop spending money and do without all of the things you really want in order to make your life better don't live in the real world. We spend money virtually every minute of our lives. It is impossible to not spend. The real issue is not that we spend money, but how we spend, that makes all of the difference.

Those who retired in 2001 and 2002 realize what I am talking about. Many have had to suffer through the pain of seeing 50 percent, or more, of their retirement nest egg disappear in the falling stock market. And, if we learned anything from the tragedy of the terrorist attacks in 2001, it is that we have no idea how long we have on this planet. We should hope for the best, but we should not take anything for granted.

Being an uncontrolled spender is also not the answer. Being a smart spender, and saving money on everything you buy, will help you add tens of thousands of dollars of increased cash flow to your financial plan today and into the future.

Introduction

I've tried to cover some of the major areas of personal finance where families make many of their biggest financial mistakes. But this book is much more than a guide to avoiding financial trouble. These strategies will help you to actively build wealth. No matter how much money you earn at your job right now, or what past financial history you are trying to overcome, the life you want can be yours if you learn these simple, but very smart financial management techniques.

This book evolved over several years. I did not intend for it to take as long as it did to complete, but, in retrospect, I am glad I had the opportunity to refine my ideas and strategies through many economic cycles and events. Our family has grown quite a bit and been through many ups and downs during my writing of this book. We've added two more children to our family, bought and sold homes, been through serious financial crisis, including job loss, too much debt, and costly medical expenses. My wife and I have gone toe-to-toe with collectors and collection agencies, saved our home from foreclosure, and lived with financial uncertainty and stress. As tough as life got at times, I feel those experiences have greatly enhanced our money management skills as a family, and my ability to relate to a wider range of real life financial situations and decisions.

If you take just one thing from reading this book, it is this simple truth: You are completely responsible and in control of your money decisions. You do not have to be a victim of the financial system and you can prosper if you take your responsibility seriously. If you are willing to make some simple changes to how you handle your money, you can be successful beyond anything you can imagine. So let's get started and I'll show you how to *Spend Your Way to Wealth*.

1

$ $ $ $ $ $ $ $ $ $ $ $ $ $ $ $ $ $ $ $ $ $ $ $ $ $ $ $ $ $

Consumers Are King

". . . you are either earning money or spending it."

You have much more power in the marketplace than you think. You, as a consumer, actually have ultimate power to decide whether or not businesses continue to exist.

Based on past experiences, you may have a hard time believing that this is true. It's easy to get the feeling that we consumers are the servants and the merchants are the masters. Personally, I believe customer service is at an all time low. There are many contributing factors but, I think this is mostly due to the fact that there are so many businesses spending very little time or resources on good training of employees.

True, some business owners have simply gotten fat and happy and have lost touch with reality. They have forgotten who makes it possible for their businesses to continue to prosper. Luckily, I have found these shopkeepers are few and far between.

I believe that most business owners want to provide a good buying experience from start to finish and they genuinely understand the importance of creating long-term, on-going relationships with their customers in order to stay in business. Unfortunately, it seems something is getting lost in the translation. I fault inadequate training, the hiring of inexperienced and unmotivated employees, and a lack of clear leadership when it comes to providing a good customer experience.

What you must remember is that you have a right to demand a great experience every time you shop. In addition, you have the right to demand the highest quality service and merchandise for the lowest possible price.

Believe me, if you and I stopped shopping at stores that offer poor quality merchandise or bad service, and if others acted with the same commitment, merchants would have no choice but to make changes or go out of business. It has happened many times in history.

Our power as consumers is limited by our willingness to take action. Most people will not act when they feel prices are too high or a product is inferior. How many times have you eaten a sub-par meal at a restaurant because you didn't want to make a fuss? Have you ever winced when someone, maybe a spouse, brought something to the attention of a waiter or a store manager? Have you ever told a spouse not to make a big deal about something you were clearly not happy with?

COMPLAIN TO THE RIGHT PEOPLE

Often, the only action we ever take is to complain after the fact. Americans love to gripe. Prices are too high; service is terrible; quality is inferior. The problem is, the complaining is not directed at the right people. Complaining to friends and family after you leave the store will do no good. You must exercise your right to super service and low prices when you are face to face with the merchants who are really in a position to respond to the complaints and make things right. If you don't give the merchant the opportunity to fix things, you'll never really know if you should go back to the store. Actually, telling a store's owner about a problem is doing them a favor. The only way to improve something is to make someone in charge aware of a problem.

If the business owner does not respond to a complaint or a request to your satisfaction, then you can make an intelligent decision about returning to the store in the future. But, if you don't give him that chance, you are the ultimate loser in the deal. You've paid too much or gotten bad service and the only people who know about it are your immediate family or friends. What can they do to make you happy? They can't get your money back for you or re-cook the meal.

How many times have you thought that the price of automobiles is ridiculously high? How can automobile manufacturers and dealers sell a vehicle for $25,000, $30,000, $40,000, or much more? For the same reason a cup of coffee now sells in most places for, like between $1.50 and $2? The gourmet coffee drinks cost as much as an entire meal used to cost not that long ago. Talk about a markup! This is a cup of flavored water selling for several dollars. The reason is clear and the blame cannot be put on the merchants for being greedy. The job of a merchant is to get the highest price possible. I'm sure you have heard the term, "what the market will bear." Cars sell for $30,000 because people are willing to pay $30,000. Cups of coffee sell for several dollars because we, "the market," agree to pay that much.

I submit that the overall feeling of powerlessness in the marketplace that consumers feel is a fallacy. If consumers took proper action when they thought they were paying too much or were receiving inferior quality or service, our true power in the marketplace would be felt.

Consumers are King for one major reason. This reason is the foundation of the American Economic System: Competition. Never has competition been greater, in all industries, than it is right now. Competition among merchants for your business gives you great power and leverage.

We no longer live in a world where a town has just one general store, one doctor, one cobbler, and one gas station. Unless you live in a very small town, it is virtually impossible for you not to have at least ten choices of where to buy each and every product you purchase.

Not only do you have choices but, also these choices are begging you to give them a chance to serve you. This is what gives you the upper hand when it comes to demanding low prices and high quality. You can choose who gives you service. Demand what you want or find someone else who will deliver what you want. Realize you will be a shopper for the rest of your life and vow to become a smart one.

ARE YOU A SMART SHOPPER?

How do you know if you are a smart shopper? Ask yourself these questions: When I make a purchase, do I question salespeople or business owners about the price and the quality of the products I am buying? Or, do I become a silent spectator? Can I ask intelligent questions about items I am shopping for or do I just believe the sales and advertising material's claims? Have I ever overpaid for something simply because I felt I had no choice or I didn't want to make a fuss?

An uninformed consumer normally has no choice but to believe and follow the suggestions of salespeople. Thus, the uninformed consumer is easily led down the path to paying more for virtually everything she buys. By just overpaying one dollar a day for thirty years, you will throw away $10,950.00. Not to mention the interest on that money for thirty years that may compound your loss to in excess of $30,000 to $50,000 over that thirty-year period.

The human tendency to be a creature of habit, who dislikes change, allows us to put up with inferior service and higher prices. For some people it is very awkward and inconvenient to shop at an unfamiliar store. Even if service is not quite the best or prices are just a little higher at the store you are used to shopping at, your tendency may be to stick with the tried-and-true.

There are people who will travel miles out of their way, passing store after store that could sell them the same exact products, often at cheaper prices, simply because they are so comfortable at their favorite stores. Loyalty to a shopkeeper is wonderful, if the shopkeeper proves his loyalty to his customers by providing the highest quality for the lowest prices.

One of the most glaring examples of unreturned loyalty I can think of is when long-distance telephone service was deregulated and AT&T began to face hundreds of competitors offering consumers much cheaper long-distance rates. In spite of the lower rates, and no difference in quality, it took years for people to start switching away from AT&T simply because of its reputation in the industry. Even though AT&T was often charging—and to this day still charges some residential customers—double the price for the same long-distance service, people were reluctant to leave AT&T because this was the company that had always provided the service. Habit and fear of change on the part of consumers kept AT&T in the position of still owning the majority of the long-distance market even though the company charged higher prices than competitors until very recently.

It is a great lesson for all business people. Build a reputation for delivering high quality service and merchandise and you can build a loyal clientele that will be willing to pay more for your services year after year. This is especially true if your clientele refuses to educate itself about your competition.

LACK OF PLANNING WILL COST YOU

Sometimes it is our own laziness that costs us money. How often have you paid double for a soda or a gallon of milk because the convenience store was on the way home, while the grocery store, where prices would most assuredly be less, was a couple of miles out of the way?

Failure to plan large expenditures is also one of the major drains on your savings account. For example, when do most people shop for tires? When they have a flat. Right? Usually, you are on your way to somewhere important and you find yourself on the side of the road with a flat tire.

The next thing you know you are at the tire store being told that not only should you replace the flat tire but the other three are bald as well and very dangerous to drive on. Not only that, but usually you are told your tires are out of alignment and the store cannot warranty new tires put on a car that is out of alignment. Alignment service is on sale today though, just $150 with the purchase of four of the $80 tires. By the way, the service technician also noticed a leak coming from your shocks.

Have you ever been in this situation? I have. Six hundred dollars and six hours later I left the store feeling as powerless and foolish as I had ever felt in my whole life.

Now, the real question here is, who is to blame? Consumers who feel powerless will undoubtedly blame the store for "ripping them off." They will say, I had no choice. I needed to get tires so I could get to work. That's what I said.

Indeed, in this situation the uninformed, stressed-out consumer does not have much of a choice. The reason, though, has nothing to do with the tire store. It has everything to do with poor planning. Had the consumer shopped for tires in advance and known about $40 tires that lasted just as long as the $80 tires, $160 would have been saved. Mr. Consumer also missed the 50 percent off the cost of tire alignment coupon that was mailed to his home by the same tire store because he throws away all of his "junk-mail" immediately. More on "junk-mail"—or as I call it, "money in the mail"—coming up later.

The time to shop for tires, or any product or service, for that matter, is before you actually need the item. Once you are in an emergency situation, whether it is car trouble or simply the fact that you haven't eaten all day and you are starving, you are forced to purchase the first available item to solve your immediate dilemma. There is no time to shop intelligently when you are hungry or broken down on the side of the road, stressed out because you are missing an important appointment. You will find yourself at the mercy of the merchants.

EDUCATE YOURSELF TO BUILD WEALTH

Yes, it takes a little work to save money and build wealth. It's not hard work. Think of it this way. You could generate savings of up to 50 percent or more of what you earn a year by doing less work than you do at your job. You must understand this important concept. It is possible for you to easily save $10,000 to $100,000 or more, each year. In fact, the less you earn each week at your job, the higher the percentage of savings you could create. A savings of $300 a year is of much greater value to someone who only earns $15,000 a year than it is to someone who earns $80,000 a year.

By educating yourself on little more than the basics, current prices and choices available, in all cases, you will save money. Did you know if you choose a certain color of car you could pay more? Supply and demand dictates prices. If a dealer sells more red cars than blue ones, guess which ones will cost more? So, when the car salesman asks you, "Which color do you like?" ask him which is the most popular color and which is the least popular color. By choosing a less popular color, you might save $500 to $1,000, or more. One simple question that takes ten seconds to ask could save you $500 to $1,000. It is that simple. When you start saving $100 a minute, then you will know what real consumer power is.

Hopefully you are starting to see the direction in which we are going here. But you can only build wealth if you are willing to ask the questions, do some homework, and prepare yourself.

My prevailing message in this book is very basic. You will be spending a lot of money during your lifetime. No one has ever disagreed with me on that point. I will go one further. You will spend almost all of your income this year and every year. As of this writing, the average American saves about one percent of his net income each year. Out of every $10,000 you earn, if you are average, you will save a whopping $100. My goal is to help you turn your $100 into $10,000, or more.

Every time you turn on a light in your house or open the refrigerator you are spending money. So, I think it is safe to make this bold claim. In life, you are either earning money or spending it. Unless you come up with a way to drastically increase your earning power beyond that annual 2 to 5 percent raise your employer gives you, the only other realistic way to generate cash flow for your family immediately, without investing money, is to save more money, starting today.

By taking control of not only your spending habits, but the entire system that you use to purchase things and spend money, you will actually be able to create wealth by saving money on every purchase you make and re-directing those savings into wealth-building vehicles such as investments.

Consider this: Do you stop every morning for a cup of coffee, a soda, a donut, or anything else on the way to work? Supposing you, like most people, work between two hundred fifty and three hundred days a year. By spending just $1 every morning (very cheap these days), you have decreased your wealth by $250 to $300. Had you not stopped two hundred fifty times last year for the morning coffee, you would have had two hundred fifty more dollars in your pocket to invest, save, or do something good with.

Many people get my message wrong when they first hear it. I don't begrudge you breakfast at your favorite restaurant every morning. What I am saying is, if you have not included that daily purchase in an overall spending plan, then you will be one of those who is shocked at the end of every month. Have you ever said to yourself when paying bills or balancing your checkbook, "Where does all the money go?"

Most working people will earn in excess of one million dollars during their careers. If that is true then why are there so few millionaires at retirement time? Why do more than 90 percent of Americans need some form of government assistance to subsist after retirement? I've got to use it here . . . you knew it was coming. It is such an overused expression, but so appropriate to this subject: These people didn't plan to fail. They failed to plan. I don't care if you make $1,000,000 a year. Unplanned and spontaneous spending, which leads to over-spending, will leave you bereft of a great deal of potential wealth.

I do not advocate budgeting in this book. Budgets do not work, as we will discuss in chapter 2. But I will show you how to plan your household spending, just as any successful business plans its spending to the dollar, for maximum savings and most efficient use of available funds. With proper planning, you could easily improve the quality of your lifestyle by fifty to one hundred times or more.

CREATIVE SAVING

Of course, there is another piece to the puzzle. Saving money on everything you purchase is part one. Part two, and what I consider the more difficult accomplishment of the two for most people, is doing something creative and valuable with the savings.

Unfortunately, some people have a hard time seeing savings as income. For example, if you buy a can of beans at the grocery store and save a dollar on that can of beans because you used a coupon, technically you have earned one dollar. Better yet you have earned one dollar, absolutely tax-free.

The grocery store would have normally earned that dollar if not for the coupon. Imagine you went into the store with a ten-dollar bill in your pocket to buy a can of beans. Let's say the can of beans costs $1.10. Using your coupon, you buy the beans, and instead of walking out of the store with $8.90 in your pocket, you walk out with $9.90. You feel great. You only paid 10¢ for the beans. What do you do now? Take that dollar and buy an over-priced soda on the way home at the convenience store, or do you put the dollar into a savings account or investment?

I will give you a hint. Most people make the mistake of buying the soda. Get that savings out of your hands as quickly as possible or the two of you will soon be parted! Invest the money. Hide it inside of a mason jar and bury it in the back yard if you have to. It is OK to spend the money on something that is needed and planned. Just don't spend the money frivolously. If you find a way to save just one dollar on something you buy every day you'll have an extra $365 in your savings account at the end of the year.

"Big deal," some of you would say, "a whole, $365? Wow!" First of all, to many people, that amount is a great deal of money. But, what if I told you that saving just $365 a year could put several thousand dollars into your pocket over a lifetime? For example, if a home mortgage payment was $365 a month for thirty years and one extra mortgage payment was made each year, you could easily eliminate seven to ten years of payments from the mortgage, which would save you thousands of dollars in interest. The $365 dollars a year could put $10,000 or more in your pocket over a number of years. Your morning donut on the way to work begins to seem a little too expensive when you start to look at the big picture, doesn't it?

When you hear people talk about working smarter rather than harder, this is what they are talking about. It is a matter of making smart spending decisions. Our system is designed to pit the advertisers and sellers of merchandise against the consumer. It is an adversarial relationship by design. Most stores don't post their wholesale prices on the wall so you know what their markup is. Few merchants tell you how low they are willing to go on price at the start of sales negotiations. Knowing all of this, do you see how important it is for you to be prepared when you go out into the marketplace?

OVERCOMING THE CURRENT ENVIRONMENT

Most people go through life blaming others for their misfortune and lack of riches. Success starts with you making the decision to do things a little differently than usual. But, I am not going to tell you that it will be easy to break old habits or learn new strategies overnight. It will take effort on your part.

Most people are simply products of their environment. In an environment where consumer debt continues to increase out of control, personal bankruptcies are at record high levels, and the average person saves less than 1 percent of what they earn, how can anyone learn to build wealth? The vast majority of consumers are in survival mode. They live week to week and, paycheck to paycheck.

Many people feel like victims when it comes to the subject of their personal finances. I am here to tell you that you do not have to continue to feel that way. No matter how intimidated you may feel right now, before you are done reading, you will have a new attitude of empowerment. It is your right. You are in control of the marketplace and your financial destiny. If you truly want to make a difference in your life financially, you can do so. Remember this important statement, as you will read it often in this book: It is not how much money you earn but how much money you keep.

The bottom line here is that the free market system is set up in such a way as to do everything possible to separate you from your money. Either you keep a big percentage of your hard-earned money and do something constructive with it or you give it away to a merchant. The great thing is, the decision is totally up to you. You are a consumer and, "Consumers are king!"

2

$ $

Budgets Are Like Diets

"You have got to want to make a difference in your life. I mean, really, deep down, you have got to want to be wealthy."

Telling people not to budget is pretty much unnecessary. Just as Americans, on average, don't save very much money, they rarely do any significant planning of their expenditures either.

Even the most simplistic form of financial planning—you know it as budgeting—is done only on occasion. Arguments between couples over money usually lead to someone laying down the law that overspending must stop. "From now on," so the speech goes, "you will not spend any more of our money on (insert here whatever it is that started the argument)." I hope not, but, unfortunately, money problems are the number one reason people give for divorcing in our country, so the fact is, this conversation is all too common. Even if money problems are not the main cause of frustration in a couple, they make a convenient excuse on which to blame the problems. Even small financial challenges can be the spark to ignite a relationship-ending situation. At best, large amounts of stress build up inside everyone involved. Either way, money problems lead to broken families, which is not a good thing.

Budgets are truly like diets. Most people start with good intentions. At least they realize something has to be done about their financial situation. The challenge with budgets is, like diets, they are usually based on depriving yourself and your family of things that you want and normally purchase.

Budgets are not based on getting the most for the dollars spent either. The science of "doing without," the tool used to teach most of us money management as children, is neither an enjoyable way to increase a family's wealth nor a very successful program in the long run. It often leads to resentment and envy of other people and families who seem to have more of everything, and this is never a healthy result.

There is also a psychological factor involved with being told not to do something. I'm not a psychiatrist, but I can tell you that lots of people have a problem with being told they can't stop for their morning cup of coffee anymore or they will have to eat the generic cookies rather than their favorite chocolate chip cookies; worse yet, there will be no cookies purchased at all because, "we just can't afford them."

Budgets also get tiresome and people forget the spending rules. The urge to "impulse-buy" things we are depriving ourselves of becomes greater the longer we deprive ourselves. An every-once-in-a-while splurge will begin to take place more and more often until the original budget plan is totally forgotten. As with a diet, one donut today leads to another tomorrow, and so on. Two extra dollars spent today can easily lead to three over-budget dollars spent tomorrow.

It takes great discipline to do without something you want, especially if you are used to having it. Most of us just are not strong enough to overcome our natural urges to have things over a long period of time. Eventually you give in to your desires and then feel guilty about it. Instead of depriving ourselves, we need to find a way to face our present spending patterns, and plan for future spending, which allows us to continue to partake of the things we really enjoy.

A BUSINESS PLAN FOR YOUR FAMILY

The best way to succeed at eliminating debt and building wealth, without depriving yourself and your family of the things you want in life, is to approach your annual spending exactly as a successful business would. A business does not fly by the seat of its pants when it comes to spending money—at least the businesses that are around for a long time do not. I have worked for businesses that have literally spent themselves right out of business. So, I know firsthand that working without a structured spending plan and realistic financial goals is a prescription for failure for businesses and for your household.

A family is really no different than a successful business. The day I started running my family's spending with a business attitude things began to change drastically for the better. I felt I finally had a real grasp of where our hard-earned money was going before it actually went away. You see, most people don't realize they are having money problems until they are in serious trouble. By then it can be too late to do anything constructive to change the situation. Being able to see where your money needs to go, before you pay a single bill, will allow you to re-direct other spending to take care of the most important things first.

The worst way to handle your family spending is to go through the month oblivious to what bills you are paying and how much you are spending. Then, once you get your bank statement and realize you don't have as much in the bank as you thought, you try to recreate the month's spending and deal with more bills and a lack of money at the end of the month. What if you get to the end of the month and you are out of money? This happens all too often for most families. This problem is so common, they write songs about it. Have you heard the country song, "Too Much Month at the End of the Money?"

I mention families quite often in this book because I know the majority of my audience will be families. But, I want to be clear to my single friends who are reading this that you are actually in a better position to begin spending your way to wealth because you can make changes more easily. Also, you probably don't have the expenditures on a weekly, monthly, and yearly basis that a family will have.

On the other hand, while it is true that a single person can make changes more quickly than a married couple, single people are also in the paradoxically precarious position of having more discretionary income. If you do not have children in your household, you may have an additional $5,000 a year, or more, at your discretion, which you could easily throw away without proper, businesslike spending strategies and a realistic spending plan.

You do not need to have a degree in accounting to accomplish what I am talking about, as you will see. You can run your family spending on a pad of paper. The keys to success are planning, organization, and consistent record keeping, in addition to a commitment to the goal of building wealth for your family's future.

Planning is the most crucial aspect of creating a good spending plan and often the toughest part of the job. Getting started is difficult and, when it comes to taking a detailed look at your family spending habits, it can be painful as well. To plan well you must have honest information about the project you are planning. Since your spending is the subject, you've got to know the facts about everyone's spending habits, including your own.

When I first went through this exercise, I disliked looking at all the money we were spending. I could not believe it. It took writing everything down on paper and adding up all the bills and expenditures to realize we were not saving a penny. In fact, if things continued as they were going, we not only would have zero savings but would also actually go deeper and deeper into debt. This normally happens when people outspend their income. And there is no income you can't outspend. When you start outspending your income you start to borrow money from credit cards, banks and other sources, usually at very high interest rates. Once you start to do that, the fall into financial oblivion is accelerated. You find yourself trying to stretch the same income to pay all of your regular bills plus the added burden of interest.

When I looked closely at our family spending, I expected to find lots of frivolous expenditures on things that we really did not need. But I was shocked to find that what we were buying was necessary. I mean, I don't have to tell you that it costs a lot of money just to cover the basic essentials of life, let alone any luxury items. Most families are not failing financially because they are spending money on fancy cars and elegant wardrobes. The problem is they are overspending on every item they buy so there really is no money left over for any thoughtless splurges. And if this family does happen to save money on some purchases, the savings are soon lost to overspending as well.

Taking a very close look at your essential purchases and how much money will be needed to take care of those purchases on a monthly and annual basis will open your eyes to exactly how much money you will need to earn just to cover your expenses. This will also show you whether you will have anything left over for discretionary spending. My plan is for you to know all of this information before your year starts, not after you discover that you don't have the money to cover the expenses of the vacation you took last month. It is too late at that point.

What you have done in the past is not important. The best way to start to move your family finances in a positive direction is to create a realistic spending plan that you can use to manage your finances going forward. The idea is to project, or forecast, your future expenses and income over the next twelve months. One of the best ways of doing this is to use past income and expenses as a guide to the future. Of course, you will take into account any potential changes that might take place in the year ahead. For example, your spouse might finish a training course or college and qualify for a raise in salary at work. Or, a child may be leaving home for college, which will lead to increased, or possibly decreased expenditures. Maybe you are planning to purchase a new home or a car. Perhaps a newborn is on the way. All of these life changes will impact your spending plan, so it is important that you take a hard look at not only the past year of income and spending, but, also, what may happen to change things in the coming twelve months.

THE SPENDING PLAN WORKSHEET

To help you create a spending plan, I've included a sample Spending Plan Worksheet. That way, you get to see the monthly fluctuations in your spending patterns that will help you plan your spending more accurately. We also offer an interactive planning worksheet on our Web site located on the Internet at *www.mikeshow.com*, along with several other financial planning tools. I have found it helpful to include each month of the year and extend out for twelve months. Your worksheet does not have to be exactly like the one included here, but it is recommended that your worksheet have as much of the same information as possible. It should include room for:

➤ Income and Expense categories listed down the left side of the sheet.

➤ Months of the year headings across the top of each column.

➤ Rows at the bottom of the sheet for totaling each column's expenses and another row below it to calculate your net surplus or loss after you subtract total expenses from total gross income.

➤ A column at the far right-hand side of the worksheet to total each category for the year.

If you have a computer, there are many fine software programs that can be purchased inexpensively or that are available for free on the Internet that can make the chore of setting up a spending plan much easier. Excel is perfect for setting up a worksheet if you know how to use it. If you've bought your computer in the past three to five years, chances are you have a financial program preloaded onto your computer that includes a budget worksheet of some sort. If you do not have "bundled" financial software, I suggest you visit your local software retailer for a good basic budgeting program or search on the Internet using key search words such as *budgets* or *budgeting*. Also, most major banks offer programs on their Web sites.

Several software programs will allow you to track your expenses throughout the year. Some of these tracking programs can even be used to help prepare your taxes, assuming you keep the system up-to-date throughout the year. If you do use it to prepare your taxes, some or all of the cost may be tax deductible depending on the prevailing tax laws at the time you are reading this. Always double-check tax questions with a certified tax preparer or at *www.irs.gov.*

If you don't have a computer, use some paper and a ruler to create a worksheet, or do what I did: Buy a standard bookkeeping tablet in the office supply section of any retail store. It will already be set up for you to input expense and income information. In the end, you will actually have two worksheets: the spending plan worksheet, where you will project your expected income and expenses for the upcoming year, and a second one set up the same way, where you will track your actual income and expenses. These two sheets will allow you to compare to your planned income and expenses. You can combine the information from both onto one worksheet if you wish. Do whatever works best for you to help monitor your plan against what is really happening throughout the year.

Let's get started and we'll begin to create a first draft of your spending plan.

TOTAL GROSS INCOME	Jan	Feb	Mar	Apr
Wages, Salary, and Other Income				
Fixed Expenses				
Income Taxes				
Federal Income Tax				
Social Security Tax				
Medicare Tax				
Other taxes				
Savings				
Personal				
College Fund				
Retirement Fund				
Employer's Contribution to 401k Plan				
Emergency Fund				
Investments				
For Future Purchases				
(Like a Car or a Home)				
Housing				
Mortgage/Rent				
Property Taxes				
Insurance				
Auto Insurance				
Life Insurance				
Homeowner's Insurance				
Health Insurance				
Dental Insurance				
Disability Insurance				
Legal Insurance (Pre-Paid Legal)				
Credit Insurance				
Loans				
Installment Loans				
Other Fixed Expenses				
Child Care				
Car Payments				

Budgets Are Like Diets

May	Jun	Jul	Aug	Sep	Oct	Nov	Dec	Total

Spend Your Way to Wealth

Variable Expenses	Jan	Feb	Mar	Apr
Heat/Electricity				
Water/Garbage				
Telephone				
Cable				
Groceries				
Credit Card Payments				
Gifts				
Medical/Dental				
Public Transportation				
School Lunches				
School Supplies				
Pet Food and Supplies				
Home Repair and Maintenance				
Discretionary Expenses				
Eating Out				
Videos/CDs				
Clothing				
Recreation				
Vacation(s)				
Education				
Newspapers/Magazines				
Haircuts/Beauty Shop				
Alcohol/Tobacco				
Charity/Church Giving				
Children's expenses				
Allowances				
Auto Repair and Maintenance				
Unexpected Expenses				
Add Your Own Categories:				
TOTAL EXPENSES				
SURPLUS OR LOSS (Subtract Total Expenses from Total Gross Income)				
EXTRA INCOME NEEDED				

Budgets Are Like Diets

May	Jun	Jul	Aug	Sep	Oct	Nov	Dec	Total

EXPECTED GROSS INCOME

At the top of the worksheet, start with all of your expected gross income. Income is a good, positive place to start. Many budgets will ask you to list your net income, that is, income after paying taxes. The reason I suggest you list your gross income is because we will be listing taxes as an expense item. In my opinion, by only focusing on net income, we totally discount the big dollars we pay out of each paycheck in the form of taxes and other payroll deductions. Start with your paycheck stub, which should detail your income and expenditures for income taxes and benefit expenses. Doing this will be a big eye opener for you, if nothing else. It is also a good idea to make sure the correct amount of money is being deducted from your pay. Don't assume mistakes are never made in your company's payroll office. Learn what amounts should be taken out and double-check each payday. Most people simply look at their net pay amount and never give a second thought to the other items. Remember, you are reading this book because you want to set yourself apart from the crowd, financially. Take some extra interest in the most important document you receive each month—your pay stub.

There is action you can take to reduce the amount of income taxes you pay, especially if you are overpaying your taxes, as people mistakenly do out of fear of being audited. By including taxes that you pay out of your hard-earned income in your spending plan as expenses, you will see the real impact of taxes on your family's financial future.

Gross income can include income from any source such as your job, Social Security payments, investment income, or income from a small, home-based business. This is where you would include your garage sale income. I personally like to list the subcategories under each main section. Under gross income, I would list all the ways in which I generate income each month. If one of your sources of income changes, the spending plan can be adjusted easily. I suggest you also add a line item at the bottom row of the worksheet called Extra Income Needed, but you will not input any numbers until you finish detailing your regular income and expenses and calculate the bottom line. The Extra Income Needed line will include income that you propose to earn each month in order to meet or surpass your monthly expenses if you find you are in a negative financial position.

EXPENSES

Now that you have your income listed, begin to think about and list your spending for the upcoming year. Again, there is no need to be fancy, just get everything you can possibly think of down on paper. I have tried to include as many common categories as possible, but every family is different and you may need to add items that are particular to your situation.

If you are stumped on how much to plan to spend in each area, here are some nationally recognized general guidelines for spending in various categories. Most lenders would consider these expense ratios to be within acceptable limits. Housing costs should not exceed 35 percent of your monthly income. Transportation should not take more than 20 percent of your monthly income. Other expenses can account for another 35 percent of your income, leaving 10 percent for savings. This is an ideal situation, but it should be a goal for you. Most lenders will look for these ratios as part of your qualification for a credit card or loan. If you know you are going to be outside of these guidelines before you even start, don't give up. You are not alone. Complete the spending plan and then you can make some decisions on where and how to get your spending back within acceptable limits.

A great way to start finding past expenses is to go through your checkbook and credit card statements for the past year. So much of what we buy is done at the spur of the moment it is easy to forget what we've purchased.

Be sure to include the small, daily expenses like cups of coffee, sodas, lunches, newspapers, and the like. The big expenses like rent or mortgage payments are easy. It is the small expenses, usually paid for with cash or credit cards that can sneak up on you and cause potential problems. Remember, our initial goal is not to look for things to eliminate. We just want to list as much as possible to see if all of your expenses are truly possible considering the income that exists to support the expenses. Can you continue to run the business of You, Inc., as you have been doing with the current income, or do changes have to be considered? Every good business owner asks that question constantly and so should you. Get as detailed as possible with your list. Input your monthly expenses in each category.

There are three broad categories of expenses. First, regular expenses such as the mortgage or rent payment, insurance, car payments, garbage, sewer, property taxes, and other regularly scheduled monthly expenses, are known as fixed expenses. Theses expenses are the same, month after month, throughout the entire year. Often, they remain the same year after year.

Second, you will have variable expenses such as the telephone bill and other utility bills. These are basically the same from month to month, but they do fluctuate.

Last, you have discretionary spending. These are the purchases that are up to you and include everything from clothing to home improvements, dining out, entertainment, and even furniture.

First, list all of your fixed expenses. The amount due on each of these bills will most likely be the same as they were last year. Your mortgage payment is probably the same unless you have moved or had a property tax increase, or maybe the mortgage insurance requirement was dropped and your payment may have gone down. If you have an adjustable rate mortgage, pay close attention to any increases that may have occurred in your mortgage payment. In fact, you should plan for the worst-case interest rate increase to be on the safe side. If your mortgage has an annual increase ceiling of, say, 2 percent, for example, factor a possible increase of 2 percent of your mortgage payment into your plan, especially if the current financial situation favors increases in interest rates. Also, make note of what would happen if the interest rate and your payment were to drop and how it would affect the cash flow in your spending plan. Now you are doing some planning. A spending plan allows you to keep an eye on your long-term debt. Long-term debt is where interest can quietly eat a giant hole in your future wealth.

In examining your variable expenses, go through your list of bills very carefully. If you have not kept very good records in the past, it would be helpful to start now by listing your bills as they come in the mail. This is also a good time to take a close look at your bills. There may be mistakes on several of them.

You should make it a habit of doing more than just looking at how much is owed and writing out a check each month. Look for discrepancies on telephone and credit card bills, and especially in hospital and medical bills.

Electricity bills can be wrong also. My wife and I once lived in an apartment where the meter reader for the electric company was reporting electric use for our apartment but was reading our neighbor's meter and vice versa. Guess who was getting overcharged? This could have gone on unnoticed forever. If we were not sensitive to our expenses we would have never suspected that such a mistake was possible. Mistakes like this happen all of the time so you must look at every bill you receive in detail to make sure no mistakes are being made and costing you extra money. Remember, the person reading the utility meter is not paying your bills. The vested interest in the reading being correct is yours. If someone does not do his or her job correctly and it costs you money, you are the one who is getting hurt financially.

Depending on how you earn a living, your income tax expense might be fixed or variable each payday. If you are a salaried employee, chances are your income taxes will be the same each time you are paid. Someone who works on a commissioned basis could have varying income amounts each payday and, therefore, the amount they pay in federal taxes will vary with each paycheck. So, computing this expense may be as simple as taking the categories listed on your paycheck stub and copying the numbers over to your spending plan, or you may have to do some estimating in order to come up with some numbers. If you do have variable income from month to month, and you expect your income will be close to last year, you could take the total amount of income tax you paid last year and divide that number by twelve to get a monthly tax expense estimate and by fifty-two to get a weekly expense.

Next, compile your variable expenses. You will have to estimate your weekly, monthly, and annual spending by totaling up all of last year's bills and dividing by twelve. If you cannot find all of last year's bills, do the best you can. Don't forget to include expenses such as birthday presents for classmates of your children or friends at work. If you or your child were invited to a birthday party for someone last year, chances are you will be invited again this year. If you get together with friends once a month and bring a bottle of wine to the dinner party, estimate the cost of the bottle of wine and how many you might have to bring throughout the year.

Be sure to check your vehicles, your home, and other areas of your personal life, and anticipate expenses. For example, roof repairs, new tires to replace bald ones in two months, or replacement of some landscaping in your yard could all be potential expenses. Go so far in your planning as to actually choose a month in which the purchases will be made. Businesses do this so why shouldn't you? It really forces you to think about details. You can always move dates around as you update your spending plan. The important thing is to get the expense down on paper.

Since you are never going to remember every single expense, and there will be surprises no matter how well you plan, I suggest you add 10 percent to all of your discretionary and variable estimated expenses just to guard against the unknown. It is better to be conservative when doing a spending plan. You can always revise your numbers as you get the real figures. However, you've got to be careful about guesstimating numbers too high also. Unrealistically high spending estimates can really throw your plan off, causing you to mistakenly change other areas of your plan, such as how much income you will need and what expenses you will have to eliminate. Anytime you calculate a number, you won't be exact, of course, but, by using past history, you should be able to get fairly close to a realistic number.

ADDING IT ALL UP

Once you have your spending plan filled with real income and expenses, total your expenses for each month at the bottom of each column. Then, subtract these expenses from your gross income and calculate whether you have a surplus of money or if you are at a loss. If you find you are in the negative for any month, you should then consider the next line called Extra Income Needed. To start, think of some ways in which you can generate income in addition to your regular income in order to make up for the shortage. Be realistic but don't be afraid to challenge yourself to earn a little more than usual. Be creative in thinking of ways in which to enhance your base income from work, perhaps a spring-cleaning garage sale. Estimate income from that sale in the month in which you might have the sale. Remember, this is a plan and plans can change. Our initial goal is to design a framework for the year ahead, or we will simply wander through, as most people do today, without any ideas on what we are spending and no way to judge how we are realistically doing in relation to our income. This would leave us without a way to make adjustments to spending in relation to our income.

WHY PRE-PLANNING IS IMPORTANT

This pre-planning is very difficult for some people. Let's face it. It is easier to wait for something to happen before you spend money than it is to plan for the expense. It is not cheaper to wait, but it is easier and human nature will push you toward the easy path.

One of my financial mentors had a saying that really stuck with me and has been a great motivational force for me since the day I heard it. He said, "If you want to be successful financially, you must be willing to do now what others won't do so that you can live tomorrow like others can't live."

You have got to want to make a difference in your life. I mean, really, deep down, you have got to want to be wealthy. If you truly want the reward, you will do the work. The great football coach Vince Lombardi said, "It is not the willingness to win that makes a team great, but its willingness to prepare to win." Proper preparation is essential to anything you do.

Family finances, after your health and relationship with your God, are the most important responsibilities you have.

I realize that planning and estimating expenses is not the most fun and exciting stuff we could be spending our time doing. These are the sorts of things that many of us have to do at work. Who wants to do it at home when we are supposed to be relaxing and spending time with our family? The fun part will come soon enough for you, though. Trust me. All it will take for you to finally see the fruit of your labor is to discover something great, like you do have enough money to buy your child the exact bicycle he wants instead of having to settle for the cheap version for his birthday. Or, yes, you can afford a larger house. Not having to settle for less is what we are all about. You can have everything you desire, even on a modest income, if you are willing to do what it takes to properly plan your wealth-building program.

Step one—outlined in this chapter—is planning expenses as best you can. Of course, you are going to forget things and you certainly cannot plan the future perfectly. Unplanned expenditures are going to come up. Being as prepared as possible will allow you to face these unplanned surprises with much more confidence because you will be acting from a strong, informed position, rather than reacting from a weak and uninformed stance.

PLANNING TO SAVE

There is one section of my spending plan that I hope you will recreate exactly. It is placing your planned savings numbers near the top of the list. For most, the typical way of dealing with savings is to pay everything else first and whatever money is left over might possibly go into savings.

There are a couple of problems with that way of doing things. First, there is rarely anything left to put into savings after paying every other expense. Most people spend every bit of their net income. Number two, if there is something left after all of the bills are paid, it is too easy to spend the money on something else. If you have a planned use for every penny of your income, including any leftover or, as a business might call it, surplus, you are less likely to impulsively spend the money.

I want you to choose a definite amount of money to be saved each month. Defining your future goals and need for money to support the lifestyle you envision in the future will help you decide how much you need to put into savings each month.

The numbers are truly staggering. To retire with income of just $50,000 a year, you will need between $1,000,000 and $1,250,000 in the bank, earning an 8 percent return after taxes and inflation. Fifty thousand dollars a year to live on may seem like a lot of money to you, especially if you are just starting out, but imagine how much more expensive things will be in thirty or forty years. That amount will seem like $5,000 a year must have sounded to someone living in the 1930s. We all have our work cut out for us.

One way to make saving happen each month without fail is to enroll in an automated payroll or checking deduction plan so each month's savings amounts are automatically invested for you. These programs take the guesswork out of saving money each month and will prevent you from spending the money before you get a chance to move it into a savings or investment account.

You will also be taking advantage of an investing technique called "dollar-cost-averaging," which, research shows, is one of the best ways to invest over the long-term. Dollar-cost-averaging, while very technical-sounding, simply means that you are investing a percentage of your income on a regular, monthly basis, over several years.

According to many investment experts, dollar-cost-averaging allows you to get the most for your investment dollars because you are putting money into investments throughout the year as opposed to once a year. Once a year, lump sum investments require perfect timing or you risk investing when the market is on its way down. By investing a little bit each month, consistently, you are going to smooth out some of the large ups and downs that can and will occur in the stock market over time.

Now that you have completed your spending plan, you should have a very realistic picture of what is really happening to your hard-earned money. Any surprises? Hopefully, you are still conscious after seeing this information in black and white. You should also feel better that you have uncovered most of the year's coming expenses and can now work on where the money is going to come from to make those purchases a reality.

Armed with your spending plan, you can begin to shop for the items you will need throughout the year before you actually need them. This provides you with enough time to search for discounts, coupons, sales, and other ways of saving money that will allow you to start spending your way to wealth. Just remember, consistency of effort over time is the most important factor. Determine to stick with your plan; if you slip up and overspend one month, adjust your numbers and get right back to the plan. You are now in control of your financial future. You have a plan!

3

$ $

Coupons: The New American Currency

"If you are lucky, you are being inundated with coupons in the mail; businesses are mailing you money."

Do you use coupons? Yes? Great. You are among the 85 to 90 percent of American households that utilize coupons on a weekly basis. You have the incredible good sense to take free money when it is offered to you. You are an astute money manager and someone who cares very much about the future wealth of your family.

No? What is wrong with you? You are throwing away tax-free money, hard, cold cash and your future wealth! You can have ten times the lifestyle you have now if you would choose to properly use coupons. In my opinion, you are just being lazy and it is costing you a lot of money!

Now that I have gotten that off of my chest, let's get to the point. I hear many excuses from people as to why they don't use coupons to save money. The most common complaints I've heard about using coupons are these two: "It is an inconvenience to cut them out of the paper," and, "It is embarrassing to hold up the grocery store check-out line while the cashier counts up my coupons."

There are a host of other reasons people use to justify not using coupons, such as, "They never have coupons in the paper for items I buy"; "They look at me like I'm using food stamps"; "The stores just mark up the price of the items that have coupon savings," and so on, and so on.

Lets start with number one. Inconvenience. You know what real inconvenience is? Getting up every morning five or six days a week and putting your kids in day care to go to a job for nine hours a day to earn just enough money to get by on. Just to earn the pleasure of starting it all again next week. I think it is a much better plan to take free money from product manufacturers in the form of coupons, cut the cost of groceries and everything else you buy, then put the savings you would have given to the store without coupons into your children's college fund.

You might be laughing, but there are people who make more money a week using coupons, rebates, and other types of discounts than a lot of people earn in a week at their full-time jobs.

Right before I sat down to write this chapter, I personally saved $4.69 using a coupon at a local sub shop for lunch. It took me less than thirty seconds to save the money. That equates to $562.80 per hour. I like to work for that kind of money.

Let me ask you a question. If you were driving around one day and you heard an announcement on the radio saying that anyone who walked into ABCD Grocery Store to shop today would be handed a $10 bill. Would you go to that grocery store to get your $10? I'd be willing to bet that you would try to work a visit to that store into your schedule.

When we walk into a store armed with $10 in money-saving coupons, we are, in effect, being handed $10 by that store. As I said earlier in this book, "Either you give your money to the merchants or you keep it; it is up to you."

You may have heard of the failed attempt by a major manufacturer to discontinue issuing coupons. The test took place in three cities in upstate New York and was a huge failure. In fact, shoppers demanding their coupons back became militant, actually boycotting products made by the manufacturer in question. Needless to say, coupons are back in upstate New York.

The manufacturer in this case was responding to statistics that show that while more than $325 billion worth of coupons are distributed in any given year, only about $8 billion worth are redeemed. That represents only about a 2 percent redemption rate. Not a very successful program in the eyes of the manufacturer and a good reason to test the idea of not distributing them.

What do these numbers tell us? First, the distribution channels for the largest percentage of coupons is outdated. Manufacturers still mainly utilize newspapers to get their name-brand coupons out at the same time newspaper readership is at an all time low. The good news is manufacturers are getting a lot more creative with distribution of coupons, making it easier for shoppers to find coupons in new places through new channels.

Second, manufacturers offer a lot of coupons on items that are new or that have low sales. Especially when it comes to food, families tend to be creatures of habit, so new items aren't usually something people want to take a chance on tasting, even if they can save a dollar or more over the cost of their favorite brand of the similar product.

Trying to boost sagging sales of products is another reason coupons are created. Unfortunately, sales are usually sagging for a reason. With food, it is usually a simple matter of taste. But you can't blame manufacturers for trying a last ditch effort to carve out a following for their product since they have invested so much money into its development and marketing.

Another reason coupon use is not as great as it could be is that stores have sales of their own. In addition, many stores have created discount-buying clubs, which their regular customers can join at little or no cost and receive savings based on their amount of purchase, products purchased, and other criteria.

Stores and businesses also create their own coupons. In fact, this is the most exciting trend in the world of wealth building using coupons. As we discussed earlier, Consumers Are King of the marketplace mainly due to fierce competition. While store owners are faced with ever-increasing costs of generating new customers, they have found offering money-saving coupons is a less expensive way to get people into their store since mass mailing can be a cheaper alternative to broadcast and print media.

Even businesses that traditionally frowned on the use of coupons to drum up business, such as doctors, lawyers, and other professionals, are forced to use coupons in order to compete successfully in a very crowded marketplace.

Often, the only difference between two competing merchants is price. Quality of service and merchandise is not the big issue it once was due to technological improvements in manufacturing and delivery. Now, you have large pools of small businesses offering very similar products and services. If one is offering a lower price through the use of a coupon or a discount of some sort, all competitors will have to follow suit or risk losing customers. Just take a look at your local cellular telephone service wars and you will see firsthand evidence of this.

The key for any business is to get the customer in for the first visit, make a great impression, and then hope the human tendency to be creatures of habit sets in. Coupons get people in the door.

MONEY IN THE MAIL

If you are lucky, you are being inundated with coupons in the mail. There is no junk mail at my house. I call it "Money in the Mail." On any given week you and I are mailed hundreds, if not thousands, of dollars.

The popular thing to do is complain about so-called junk mail. If businesses were mailing checks to homes, I wonder if people would be complaining so much. In fact, AT&T, MCI, and other long-distance service providers have mailed checks to people in an effort to gain new customers. Some of these checks were for as much as $100. I received a $100 check from one of these companies and you bet I cashed it. How many of those checks do you suppose were thrown away as "junk mail" without ever being opened? Did you throw one away?

I submit that businesses are mailing you money, even if it does not come in the form of a check. If you can go to a local restaurant and save $5 with a coupon, didn't that restaurant just give you $5?

You may say, "Well, I had to eat there to save the money so it actually cost me money." I say, you would have eaten there anyway and paid an extra $5 without the coupon. Just as the people who sat next to you and behind you did. These people walked out of the restaurant with five less dollars in their pocket than you because you used a money-saving coupon. Who is smarter financially? Who is building wealth more quickly?

What you do with the savings is the really important part. The smart wealth builder is going to see that $5 savings as tax-free earned income and will invest it into an asset that will help build a solid financial future. Putting $5 a week, or any amount, away in a good investment or savings account is a great way to start doing something for your financial future.

But, in any given week, you can easily generate much more than $5 in savings. Here is where your spending plan becomes a great tool. Knowing what you have to buy allows you to search for coupons and discounts on those particular items.

Yes, businesses that mail you coupons are trying to sell you something. Why would you get upset at that, considering you have to buy things? I see this as a very mutually beneficial arrangement. Not only can I save money but also I can save time. If two competitors are mailing me sales offers, I can compare prices right from the comfort of my own home and go to the store that has a better deal. Shopping in the real world is tough work with driving, parking, searching for prices, dealing with salespeople and crowded stores. I like to shop at home. And, apparently, based on the huge success of the various home-shopping TV networks, I am not alone.

Thanks to technology, if we don't want to, we don't ever have to leave our homes to buy things. I highly suggest that you get out of the house and interact with people. It is healthy. But, there is nothing you cannot purchase over the telephone (or via the computer), from automobiles to fresh salmon from Alaska. The world is at your disposal from the comfort of your living room.

Here is another thought for you to ponder: People really don't write to each other anymore since the telephone is so easy to pick up and use, so the only other thing I usually get in the mailbox besides money-saving offers are bills. I would much rather open up a mailbox full of money than a box full of bills. I believe very strongly in this simple credo: "You are either making money or you are spending money every day of your life."

I actually feel disappointed if I don't receive some "money in the mail" every day of the week. And I think you should change your thinking about "junk-mail" also. You must become a seeker of coupons and discounts if you are ever to gain the success you want financially.

If you are still not convinced that using coupons is a smart idea, keep this thought in mind: With the increase in the use of coupons by businesses trying to build store traffic, who do you think finances the printing and redemption of coupons? People who don't use coupons, of course. You don't think the merchants are just giving that money away, do you? It is a cost of doing business and as business costs rise, so do the prices of prod-ucts. If I save $5 at the sub shop, and ten other people use the same coupon that day, the store needs to raise prices to compensate for the $50 advertis-ing expense. If you are paying full price all the time, you are subsidizing my coupon usage. Thank you very much; my family and I really appreciate your generosity; however, I think now is the time for you to wise up and get into the game yourself.

Someone once described their transformation from full-price payer to saver as simply deciding to become a "money-saving detective." The whole family has gotten involved with finding savings on things they buy every day. Now, they buy virtually nothing unless they have a way to save money on the retail price.

There are a number of strategies and techniques you should employ in addition to being on the lookout for coupons and discounts. I've listed some of the more important techniques here:

GET YOUR NAME ON AS MANY CONSUMER BUYING LISTS AS POSSIBLE

Manufacturers often do surveys to find out what you think of their products. Fill these surveys out and send them in. It is well worth the time investment, as is any survey or questionnaire that promises to reward your participation with money-saving coupons and special offers.

To show you how powerful this technique is, look at what happened when my wife simply filled out an expectant-mother survey card she got out of a major magazine. A large manufacturer of children's goods sent us a $15 discount certificate useable at any local store that sold its product. A local children's store sent us a coupon for $10 off of the price of any of its high chairs. By combining the certificate with the coupon, we saved $25 on the high chair. And that was just the beginning of what we eventually received in the form of money-saving offers over several years.

But the saving will never really end as our child begins to grow. Thanks to computers, companies can keep track of us throughout our entire lives. As our child grows older and his needs change, manufacturers will be responding to those new needs with more money-saving coupons to get us interested in other products. At least the well-run companies with the smart marketing and advertising departments will do this type of tracking. The only glitch in the process is if we move and don't leave a forwarding address. Don't ever make that mistake. It will cost you lots of money.

In the two minutes it took for my wife to complete the survey and mail it, she was able to generate hundreds of dollars, and, potentially, thousands of dollars in savings over many years on products we would have had to purchase anyway.

Even if the product in question were not something you normally would purchase, get your name on their list. Why? The reason is simple. Guess what these companies do with the lists of people who respond to their surveys, which you are added to once you respond to their questionnaire? They rent or sell the list of names to other manufacturers who are looking to do a similar promotion or possibly just direct-mail some coupons to shoppers to get them interested in their line of products.

By responding to one survey or promotion, you will be categorized by the advertising industry as a responsive consumer. Advertisers like you because, by responding, you help them do their job more effectively since they can get feedback from you about their products.

Have you ever subscribed to a magazine and then found you were receiving what seemed like hundreds of offers each month to subscribe to other magazines? The moment you become a subscriber, your name is circulated as such to other publishing companies who will then target you as a responsive magazine reader. You will receive tons of "try a free issue," offers, often for years after your original subscription request.

Your goal is to get on as many lists as possible so you receive more and more offers in the mail. This is the easiest way to get national companies to mail you money. Also, when you buy products, which include a registration card in the package, fill out the card and mail it in. This identifies you as a customer of the company and they will add you to their mailing list. And guess what they do with your name? That's right, they share it with other companies. Hey, you are really starting to catch on.

EXAMINE BULLETIN BOARDS FOR REBATES, COUPONS, AND SPECIAL OFFERS

Whenever you walk into a store, look up front for a bulletin board or coupon rack where offers are displayed. It takes a few extra minutes but can pay off handsomely if you find some offers to save money on the items you are about to shop for and buy without a coupon. This can really be a hidden treasure trove of big savings. Most people can't be bothered to spend a few extra minutes looking for ways to save money. After all, a friend might see them perusing the coupons on the bulletin board in front of the store and get the idea that they are cheap or need financial help. I say, become a "savings detective," and we will see who needs financial help down the road.

Many grocery stores in my area have installed little electronic coupon dispensers right in the aisles in front of the actual product they are trying to promote. Besides being a great distraction for the kids, it is another way for you and I to save money. How much easier can they make it for us to build a richer lifestyle?

LEAVE YOUR BUSINESS CARD IN RESTAURANT "FISH BOWLS"

Many stores, but especially restaurants, use a very simple system of building up a list of customers who have visited their store whom they can continue to target market. These establishments place a bowl or box at the cash register, or on the way out, which prompts you to enter a drawing for a free lunch or some other giveaway. It is a great idea to drop a card in these. If you don't have business cards, use small index cards that you type or hand write with your name and address on them. You may not win a free lunch but chances are great that you will receive money-saving offers from these stores in the mail several times a year.

PICK UP WEEKLY NEWSPAPERS AND OTHER FREE PUBLICATIONS

These publications like the *Thrifty Nickel* and the *Penny Saver* are everywhere, and are usually full of local business coupons. In addition to coupons, theses publications consist almost entirely of classified advertisements from individuals and businesses selling every imaginable item, from toys to cars. If you are interested in saving a great deal of money on household items like furniture and sports equipment, these are great places to look, especially if money is not very plentiful for you right now.

BUY COUPON BOOKS FROM SCHOOL CHILDREN AND ORGANIZATIONS

Besides supporting good causes, you can make out like a bandit by purchasing any number of pre-packaged coupon books, which are being sold as part of fundraising. Some of these books sell for as much as fifty dollars but contain thousands of dollars in money-saving discounts. Utilizing a "Gold C" coupon book, which we bought for $12 from our child for his school's annual fundraising event, our family saved approximately $1,200— mostly at restaurants and local merchants. You cannot match that rate of return on any other investment that I know of that is legal. And these books are so easy to use. You simply keep them in the car and you can save money on just about every trip you make.

MEMBERSHIP ALWAYS HAS ITS PRIVILEGES

Organizations, associations, churches, clubs, schools, and other similar groups that you may be a member of may have arranged for their members to get special discounts and offers from local and national merchants. Just by showing an identification card in some cases, you will receive instant discounts on your purchases.

You probably receive updates on discounts from these groups in a monthly newsletter or posted on a bulletin board at the group's headquarters. If not, call someone in charge and ask if any kind of special offers have been arranged for members. If nothing is in place, your organization's leaders are not doing a very good job in providing benefits to their members and I would bring it up at the next opportunity.

Businesses like to offer discounts to large groups because it is cost-effective; they have a targeted group for their offer and the groups tend to patronize and be loyal to merchants that are friendly to their organizations. In many cases, the group or organization will pay all the costs of advertising the discount offer to its members. This is really a great win-win-win situation for all involved. The business gets low-cost or free advertising, group members and their families can save money, and the organization is seen as doing good work by providing benefits for its members.

If you are a business owner, you should seek out as many organizations as possible and offer members some sort of discount. If you are a businessperson who regularly hands out a lot of business cards, try having some discount offer printed on your business card if you sell a product. You might offer a 10 or 20 percent discount, for example, to those who show your business card when they make a purchase. And avoid using an expiration date if you can. This will ensure that people you give your card to will hold onto it and keep it in a cherished place for future use.

READ THE INSERTS IN YOUR BILLS

Credit card companies, especially, have spent the last few years creating wonderful benefit programs for their customers and they could add new ones at any time. Other companies are also realizing the benefit of offering customers additional benefits along with their bills to soften the blow a little.

Credit cards are a subject all unto themselves. They are one of the greatest creations ever for consumers, as well as one of the most dangerous things in the world, which, if used improperly, can ruin you, your credit record, and your financial security for many years and possibly a lifetime.

Used correctly, credit cards are magical. For the purposes of our discussion, regarding you getting discount offers and coupons mailed to you, I will say that the more you use your cards, especially store credit cards, the more offers you will receive. This is simply because you are considered a regular customer. You will normally receive invitations to special sales, receive offers of additional savings if the store card is used, get free gift-wrapping, and so on.

If you can handle your credit cards properly and are not susceptible to impulse shopping, you will do very well. If you have a tendency to get into trouble with credit cards, stay away from them. The potential risk to your credit and finances far outweighs any benefits you will receive.

CALL STORES AND ASK FOR DISCOUNT OFFERS

If you are planning to shop at a store and find yourself without any coupons, you might call the store and ask if they have recently mailed any coupons out. Often, the store will get a distribution of coupons or advertisements that contain coupons to have on hand at the store. You may not have been on their mailing list but there is no reason why you can't save money also. They may either mail you the offer, or, we've actually had store clerks that we made friends with over the telephone simply hold the offer for us at their register. We just found the register and picked up our money savings. My wife and I have actually had clerks go through newspapers cutting out coupons that we had missed in order to give us a discount on items we were in the process of purchasing at full price. Now that is what I call good service!

CONTACT MANUFACTURERS DIRECTLY

Manufacturers like to hear from consumers. It helps them to become more efficient at producing products by understanding what their customers like and dislike about their products. While anyone can contact the manufacturers, I especially recommend this for families with expectant mothers. I suggest you contact companies that produce diapers, formula, baby food, and all of the other things you will need. Tell them you like their products and wonder if they have any special discount offers available. Several manufacturers have baby clubs, which they will add your name to and you will soon be receiving offers in the mail on a regular basis.

Also, check with local merchants regarding special discounts or savings programs. When my wife was expecting our second child, I remember receiving $28 in free baby items from one of our local grocers as a welcome gift for joining the store's baby club. While $28 may not sound like a lot of money to you, it was a wonderful gesture that we remember to this day. They did not have to give us anything and we still would have had to buy the usual array of baby items. That money allowed us to get more than we normally would have purchased and when it comes to your children, anytime you can do more for less, you are in a great position.

CHECK OUT THE INTERNET

If you have a personal computer, go online and you will find discount offers with every click of your mouse. Most manufacturers of any size have a Web site and usually feature money-saving rebates and coupons to entice buyers. We believe in using the Internet so much for saving money and building wealth that I have devoted an entire chapter of this book to that very subject.

ENRICHING YOUR LIFESTYLE

I hope that if you did not see the opportunity that exists to build a richer lifestyle using coupons when you started reading that you now realize what great value exists in using coupons. You see, not only are you keeping money where it belongs—in your pocket—when you use coupons and other money-saving offers, you are also enriching your lifestyle. If you use coupons, you could easily double the number of times your family can go out for dinner each year, if that is something that is important to you. Paying discounted prices allows you to afford a better quality of clothing and take better, longer vacations. Using coupons will allow you and your family to eat better food, also. You simply will be able to have more and do more by virtue of the fact that you will have more money to do things that you want to do.

These strategies for cutting expenses only work if you are willing to work at them. Once you begin to be a savings detective and you see the positive difference it begins to make in your lifestyle, you will truly wonder how you ever got along by paying full price for everything.

GET ORGANIZED

Now that I have convinced you that you should use coupons and how to get them, lets discuss organization. Organizing your coupons is just as important as using them. In fact, I believe this may be the number one reason that more coupons aren't used. Consumers are simply not organizing their coupons properly and do not have access to them when they need them. You could have hundreds of dollars worth of coupons for items you are going to buy, but, if they are stuffed in a kitchen drawer while you are at the grocery store, they are useless to you. It's like leaving your purse or wallet home. You are out of business.

Here are some ideas on organizing your coupons and discount offers properly so that accessing them when you need them is very easy. First, separate your coupons into different general categories such as grocery, restaurant, automobile service, furniture, entertainment, etc. If, like most Americans, you live in a community where everybody drives, it is a good idea to keep coupons in your car since you use them when you are out. This is especially important when it comes to coupons for restaurant savings, vehicle service, and maintenance items for your car. It is a terrible feeling to be standing in line at the local restaurant paying full price for your lunch when you know you have a free sandwich coupon sitting at home.

Grocery coupons should be categorized by type of food or product and kept in a master file. When you make your shopping list, take the coupons out of the master file for the foods and products you are going to buy. For safety sake, bring the master file with you just in case you remember an item while you are in the store that you may have left off of the shopping list. I like to put my coupons in order by expiration date.

I recommend that you make decisions on whether or not to keep coupons as you receive them in the mail or cut them out of the paper. If you stuff every coupon you receive into a drawer, it will quickly become a cluttered, unorganized mess, and a real challenge to sift through when you need a coupon for a specific item. Again, your spending plan is the perfect tool to use in deciding which coupons to keep.

The challenge of staying organized will get tougher as you increase your skills at attracting coupons to your home. But, if you have a good system to start with, staying organized will not be difficult.

It's a good idea to create several master files. Create one for groceries, one for home repairs and, of course, a master file to keep in the car for restaurant, car service, and entertainment coupons, etc. There are many coupon holders, folders, and notebooks available to help you keep them organized. Many people I know just make their own using a school notebook or a personal organizer, which includes pockets. Whatever you feel most comfortable with will work.

TRACK YOUR SAVINGS

Using coupons will quickly become part of your regular routine. You should get to the point where you feel something is missing if you are not using a coupon for just about everything you buy. Being sensitive to your spending on a daily basis is still crucial to your success. Using coupons is just one of the ways to take action by increasing your spending power and reducing your expenses.

It is also a good idea to keep track on paper all of the savings you generate through the use of coupons, special discounts, and money-saving offers. This is one of the greatest motivational tools. It will make you feel good about your efforts and will also give you an idea of how much money you have generated for your family. Yes, you are generating money for your family. Actually, you are keeping it from going into someone else's pocket, which is just as good. And, as a special bonus, the taxman does not take a piece of your hard-earned money because, as I said earlier, savings are like tax-free income. If you keep an extra dollar in savings, you don't have to pay income tax on that savings. You get to keep the full dollar.

This is a difficult concept for many to grasp, so let me explain my thoughts further. Suppose you earn $10 an hour at your job. If you go to work for an hour today, you would earn $10, less income taxes, leaving you with about $7 of $8 in net income that you would not have otherwise had. Now, suppose you to the grocery store today, armed with $10 in money-saving coupons. You would have spent $50, but, because you use the coupons, you only spend $40, leaving you with $10 you would not have otherwise had. Since no taxes are due, you get to keep the entire $10. In each case, you increased your cash flow, but using the coupons was nearly effortless and you ended up with more money in the end. Who would you consider to be smarter financially: the person who goes to work for an hour to earn $8 but then spends $50 at the grocery store without coupons, or the person who simply goes to the grocery store and buys $50 worth of food for $40?

JOIN A DISCOUNT-BUYING PROGRAM

If you really want to make saving money easy to do, you may consider becoming a member of any number of discount-buying programs. These programs make the process of getting coupons for just about anything you want and need to buy as easy as checking off a list of what you want. Clipping coupons out of the newspaper is not required when you are a member of a program such as the Be InCharge Club, Everyday Savings Club, Coming of Age, or Fun2Save.

There are companies in existence that will sell you a membership priced anywhere from $10 to $100 per year. This membership will give you access to discounts on hundreds, or even thousands, of everyday products and services. Many of these programs only offer discounts at national chain stores. While these are good programs, be sure that your local area is home to most of the stores featured in the program.

Most of the companies that market these savings programs have a grocery coupon benefit available. This service will allow you to actually pick manufacturer's grocery coupons for foods you buy every week rather than having to settle for only what is in the newspaper or magazines.

This grocery-coupon saving program is a simple system where you use a book of order forms. Inside the book you'll find a list of thousands of name-brand products from which you may choose coupons for the products your family enjoys. Using your order forms, you will mail your coupon choices to a clearinghouse which then mails you back real manufacturer's coupons that you can use in any grocery store in the country that accepts coupons. Your savings will range from 10¢ to $1 and sometimes more, depending on what is available.

Depending on the type of book you purchase, it will include order forms for a total of anywhere from $80 to $600 in grocery coupons. Once you use up all the order forms you just buy another book or renew your membership.

Some programs require you to mail in $1 or $2 plus a self-addressed stamped envelope with your coupon orders, to cover the cost of processing your order and mailing it back to you. This additional expense is more than offset by the fact that you will be sent extra coupons to cover whatever processing fee is required. For example, if the program requires you to send in $2 to process your order for $10 worth of coupons, the company will generally send you back $12 in coupons.

This is a fantastic way to get access to coupons for the foods you really buy. These programs are very smart investments. Look at the great return you will receive on your investment dollars. For an initial investment of, say, $25 to buy one of these grocery-coupon savings books, you can expect to save in the area of $300 at the grocery store. That computes to better than a 1,000 percent return on your investment. Where else can you get such a great return?

And now these discount-savings programs have set up shop on the Internet, making it even easier to generate huge savings each year using coupons. You can literally search for coupons for the items you wish to purchase and then print the coupons right on your printer.

On the Internet, you usually pay to join a buyer's club, which gives you access to the company's Web site. You are given access to order coupons a specified number of times each month for your fee. If you are using the service regularly for most of your grocery needs, these buying clubs are incredible deals. You can save thousands of dollars a year with your computer. By the way, not to jump ahead, but this is a great way to justify the purchase of a computer for your household. You can make the investment back fairly easily by using your computer to find coupons and discounts on everything you buy.

I hope you realize the incredible power we are talking about here for you, the consumer. We have literally reached the age of being able to print "money" out of our computers, legally. I challenge you to print yourself $100 in coupons this month. Take it from me, it feels great!

I do want to give you a word of warning. You are advised to check out any discount-buying business thoroughly before sending them your hard-earned money. There are many legitimate companies out there who will provide great service and give you big value for your investment. However, there are always a few rip-off artists waiting to steal from you. Proceed with caution, but please, do proceed.

A SIMPLE EXPERIMENT

For those of you who are still not convinced that coupons are going to make a difference for you financially, let me ask you to do one simple exercise: This weekend, pick up a copy of your local Sunday paper and go through it looking specifically for any and all money savings. Pick out every offer that indicates a savings amount, even for items you may not normally use. Cut them out, make a pile and, then, using a calculator, add up the savings. If it is a percentage savings, estimate what the item normally costs; estimate low just to be conservative. I challenge you to find at least $500 in savings in your $2 Sunday paper. Then, I will ask you to check how much time it took you to find that entire savings. Have you ever made $500 that quickly before in your life?

I dare to go further and say at least half of the savings you will find could be used by you and your family for items you need and buy all of the time. You may not need those items today or even this month. But, eventually, you will need to buy those items, and you will most likely do it by paying full retail price.

Once you start to see how running your personal financial affairs like a business rather than a hobby pays off in a big way, you will come to realize how important it is to do so. A good business would never pass up the opportunity to save several hundred dollars each year on all of the things the business purchases. So why are you passing up opportunities to save? Isn't your family more important than any business? Who better to work for than yourself and your family?

Here is a quick word to businesses on behalf of all of us Power Buyers: Please keep using coupons and savings offers to market your products and services to us. We really appreciate the opportunity you are providing all of us to build a richer lifestyle for our families. Yes, you could lower your prices on everything, but that is not very practical and we understand. With coupons though, only the people who are serious about improving their finances will take advantage of your generous offers and, if that allows you to continue to make these offers, that is OK with us. By the way, since we are talking, we'd really like you to improve your customer service.

I know, but it was worth a try anyway.

$ $ $ $ $ $ $ $ $ $ $ $ $ $ **4** $ $ $ $ $ $ $ $ $ $ $ $ $ $

The Perpetual Sale

"Everything in the store is for sale but not everything is on sale."

When was the last time you went into a store and there was not a sale going on?

I cannot remember being in a store where there were no "SALE" signs displayed. Merchants have been forced by competition to create what I call the Perpetual Sale. The Perpetual Sale is a state where stores must have constant sales going on in order to draw potential buyers. It is admission that their normal, everyday prices are not good enough to draw a flow of regular visitors. Every holiday, no matter how obscure, now has a sale attached to it. Every season has a sale. It seems every store is having a sale, every day.

Using the word "SALE" in almost every advertisement retailers place either in the newspaper, radio, television, and now, the Internet, has become such an accepted advertising technique that in many cases, it is, in my opinion, misleading to you and me. You have probably heard the term, "bait and switch." This is an advertising trick where only one television or car, or whatever the item might be, is advertised at a very low price. The price is set low enough to get your attention and the attention of thousands of your fellow consumers. Only one item is priced that low, not all of the inventory. Of course, there is no mention of that fact in the advertisement. Sometimes, a disclaimer is included in the advertisement, like, "while supplies last." By the time you and I get to the store, the sale item at that low, low price has "already been sold." But, good news, they have lots of similar items for just a little bit higher price. Sound familiar? Tricks like this have been used for many years. I think car dealers take the brunt of the ire for running ads like these that mislead consumers—maybe because they are very visible. But, the fact is, many merchants use this form of advertising. It is also known as using a "loss-leader." The store sometimes even loses money on the sale of the low-priced item just to buy foot traffic into the store.

When we see the word "SALE," we are conditioned to expect to pay less. But, you must be careful. We are in a market atmosphere now where the word "SALE" is used even if nothing is technically being sold at a discount. Remember, everything in a store is *FOR* sale, but not everything is *ON* sale. Stores "Going OUT *FOR* business," aren't necessarily "Going OUT *OF* business."

You could end up wasting a great deal of time if merchants use tricks instead of legitimate discounts to get you to shop at their stores. I wish the prices were so good normally that they wouldn't even need to use special gimmicks to draw us in. There are some stores that do, indeed, offer such great prices that they don't need to have sales and never do. These stores are few and far between, but they do exist.

There was a time when sales were reserved for special occasions; they were a way for a merchant to eliminate over-stocked inventory or celebrate a holiday. Not anymore. We have evolved from occasional, Special Sale Days, to an atmosphere of constant sales. Consumers now expect sale prices all the time. Which makes the entire process confusing because, eventually, you begin to wonder what a sale price is, or, whether a "SALE," really means discount prices or just business as usual. Some successful retailers have turned this phenomenon in their favor by branding their stores as places to get "discount prices everyday." Then, these stores have sales to further discount the items. If you think about it, if a discount store can mark merchandise down 50 to 70 percent, are they really a discount store in the first place?

WHAT DOES MSRP MEAN, ANYWAY?

A legitimate question to ask is whether or not the price being advertised is really a sale price. Think about it. If an article of clothing is marked down $10 for a month, doesn't the markdown price become the regular price after a week or two? Even if the price tag shows a suggested retail price of $50 and the "sale" price is $40 dollars, how long can it be for sale at $40 before the $50 retail price loses its meaning?

For that matter, what is the real story on manufacturer's suggested retail prices or MSRP? This is the price that the manufacturer "suggests" the item be sold for. But, as you know, most stores are not following the guidelines of their manufacturers because it seems everything is being sold under MSRP. Note that the price tag often reads, say, "compare at $75.00." It usually doesn't say "previously sold at $75.00," because, the chances are very high that the article has never been sold at the manufacturer's suggested retail price.

The Federal Trade Commission, in its Guide Against Deceptive Advertising, provides some guidelines when it comes to merchants using comparison pricing in their advertisements. If a merchant compares a new sale price to a former price to show a big advertised discount, "the former price has to be one which the item was openly and actively offered for sale for a reasonably substantial period of time."

Equally as confusing is when you walk into a store with "SALE" prices posted and no other prices posted with which to compare the sale price. Maybe the sale is advertised as 25 percent off. But, you have to ask yourself, 25 percent off of what price? If this is an item you have not shopped for previously, or priced before, or you have not bought this item in quite a while, you would not have a point of reference to decide if the sale price is valid. I have also found, unfortunately—and you may have found this true as well—that asking the sales clerks about a sales price or any information regarding price is not very helpful in most cases. I have found this to be especially true in chain stores and stores located in malls where the staff is young, inexperienced, and usually working part-time.

The sales clerks are often not even aware of the details of a sale. Yes, they helped put the signs out and marked down some inventory, but apparently no one told them that customers might ask questions.

Then again, when is the last time you asked a sales clerk for details about a product's former price in reference to the sale price? Either you found out previously that they don't have the answers and decided not to bother ever again, or you just see the sign and assume the sale price is a true discounted price. Taking the latter attitude will most certainly cost you some serious money over a lifetime of spending, if you take the term "sale" at its face value.

Having a reference price is the only way to successfully take advantage of truly discounted prices. You have got to know for sure that the sale price is a real, discounted price. Then you can make intelligent buying decisions.

It is interesting. If a salesperson tells us about a sale price, we are less likely to believe it. But, if a "SALE" sign is placed above a rack of shirts, we immediately assume the shirts are priced lower than normal.

THE PERPETUAL SALE VERSUS THE SMART CONSUMER

Who wins in the Land of Perpetual Sales? We do. Smart consumers. The Perpetual Sale is another victory for informed consumers. But, you can only consider yourself victorious if you use knowledge, good judgment, discipline, and your spending plan when taking advantage of legitimate sales.

This is an important point. If you are an impulsive shopper, you are especially at risk for overspending at sales. You usually end up with a lot of items you really don't need, but, in your mind, they *were* on sale. Yes, sales are wonderful opportunities to double or even triple your buying power and increase your lifestyle if you are in control. Uncontrolled spending, even for items at half price, is reducing your wealth!

Informed shoppers—I call them "Power Buyers"— know a real sale from an advertising trick 99 percent of the time. But, even the most experienced shopper has been fooled once in a while. There are some basic questions you should ask yourself before purchasing an item that is "On Sale."

➤ What was the original price? No, I am not referring to the MSRP, discussed above. I am talking about the price that the store has been selling the item at normally for the past few months. Usually that price is either handwritten or stamped on the price tag under or near the suggested retail price.

A new way to lure you to the sale racks is with signs that show a big discount like 50 percent off. But, read on and you'll see that the 50 percent discount will be taken from the original price or the MSRP and not the current price or sale price. It can be confusing trying to figure out the real discount so you have got to beware. You might spend fifteen minutes picking out your size and color only to realize it is not such a hot discount after all. In my opinion, the merchandise at most of the mall-based, larger retailers is so highly priced to begin with, that even a 50 percent discount on an item's original price is often still too much to pay for the item.

➤ How long has the item been on sale? If it has been on sale at a discounted price for a while and is still available, perhaps it will be marked down again soon. This is especially true with clothing. At the end of a fashion season—summer for example— stores must make room for their fall and winter inventory and begin to mark down the summer wear, often over

several weeks, in an attempt to reduce inventory. As each
week passes, a further reduction is implemented for remaining
inventory. By waiting, you can often save an additional 20–60
percent, or more.

➤ How long is the sale scheduled to last? Your decision-making
process on what and whether to buy today is different at a
one-day sale compared to a three-week, inventory clearance
sale. By the way, double-check to make sure a "one-day" sale
is really going to end after today. Often, a store will keep the
item at the discounted price after the sale ends. This is
especially true for end of season, inventory clearance sales.
It is less likely in situations where the store is kicking off a
new season and wants people to come in and look at the
new inventory.

You can find the answer to most of these questions by asking the store
clerks to check the schedule for the sale. They generally don't know off of
the top of their heads. Ask the manager on duty if the clerks don't know. I
have found that if they do know the information, salespeople are generally
honest about how long a sale is going to last and will even tell you if the item
is expected to be reduced further and how soon.

And for items not on sale that we wish to purchase, we have gotten
into the habit of asking if it will be going on sale anytime soon. You'd be
surprised at how many times we have been told about a sale coming up in
a week or two where our item will be discounted. The stores know this
information in advance because they have to prepare the inventory and do
the markdowns for the sale.

Also, if you buy something that goes on sale the following week, make
it a point to go back to the store and ask for the discount. A good merchant
who values your business will honor the discounted price. The store really
has no obligation to give you a refund, but you have nothing to lose by
asking and several dollars to gain.

➤ How many of the items are still in inventory? If the item you are thinking of buying is the only one left, it may not make sense to try and wait for a greater price reduction next week. Your item may be gone. On the other hand, if there are several of the same items left on the shelf, chances are better that there will be some left next week at a further reduced price. You do run the risk of missing out on the item if there is a limited inventory and the discount price is good. So you need to make a decision. If the item is a "must have," item, you may choose not to wait for further reductions.

BARGAINING FOR DISCOUNTS

Can you shop the discounted price at competitors for even greater savings? Stores that sell similar or the same merchandise don't always have sales at the same time. If store A is selling an item at 20 percent off, and store B carries the same item, ask store B if they would like to beat the 20 percent discount offered at store A to earn your business. This strategy works better with larger items like cars. In fact, many stores use an offer such as "We'll beat any price offered by a competitor by 10 percent or 20 percent." If you know which retailers have this policy, it can be very useful in helping you build wealth. An offer to always meet or beat the competition's price is an attempt to add value to a brand. However, the merchants know that the percentage of people who remember this fact and actually take advantage of it is extremely small. For most people, it would be a waste of time to drive to a competing store to get an extra 10 percent off. And I agree, depending on the price of an item, it may not be worth your time investment. But the idea is to be aware of the opportunity you have to cut your expense further, and then you can at least make an informed decision about whether or not it would be worth the effort to seek out further reductions. Maybe it is just a matter of carrying the receipt from store B with you, so the next time you visit store A, you can compare prices to see how much you could have saved. Then, in the future, you will have a reference point for buying that item. This is a must for items you purchase on a fairly regular basis.

PLAN YOUR SALE SPENDING

Are you buying for the fun of buying or is this something you really need? I love to shop but can walk away from any sale price, no matter how temptingly low, if I really don't need the item. And you should control yourself as much as possible.

Sales are great gift buying opportunities. Make it a habit of bringing your birthday and other gift buying needs list for the year with you to each sale you attend. Most people wait until the last minute to shop for gifts and almost always pay full retail price because they are under pressure to get something in a hurry. If you have a lot of gifts to buy during the course of the year, it makes sense to carry that list with you all the time. Be sure you have specific dates for when the gift will be needed and the reason for the gift listed next to the person's name on your list to make your buying decisions easier when shopping.

WHAT'S YOUR TIME WORTH?

Another great question to ask yourself is whether or not the money savings are really worth your time investment. All of the strategies mentioned above can be accomplished in a few minutes and are worth your effort. If you find that saving money is going to cost you some sizable time investment, like having to drive across town, wait in a long line, or wait for additional inventory to be delivered, I advise you to seriously evaluate whether the discount is worth your time.

Personal time investments are often lost in the quest for savings. If it costs you $5 in gasoline and two hours of your life to drive to a sale where you save $5, you are losing money. Your personal time is worth something. Most people do not put any value on their time. If you do not work in a profession where you charge customers by the hour for your personal services, it may be difficult for you to grasp this concept. Why? Well, I believe it is because of the fact that most people perceive a direct correlation between cost and actually spending money. If you "do-it-yourself," and don't actually spend money, it is seen as getting it for free, or, at a lot less than it would have cost if you had to pay an outsider for the same service.

I'll agree that you might pay less by doing something yourself instead of hiring a professional, but you do pay something for the service.

Let's do the math together. Oil changes are one of my favorite areas to make this point. The good news, in my opinion, is that automobile manufacturers are making it so difficult to do repairs on your car that more and more people are forced to let a professional do it for them. However, there are many who still choose to do it themselves. Do you really save money changing your own oil? You can get an oil change in most places for less than $15; even less if you use a coupon. If you bought the oil yourself you'd spend at least $4 to $5 on oil. Forget about the special wrench, oil pan, and funnel you'd have to buy because most do-it-yourselfers, have those already. (The first time you buy this stuff you are in for at least $20.) But, let's stick with $5 for a fair grade of five quarts of oil.

How much time does it take to change the oil on a car? When I go to the professionals, between draining the oil and adding the fresh oil and checking all of the other vital fluids, at least thirty minutes. Now, think about what you earn an hour. Let's use $10 an hour as an example. At $10 an hour, to hire you, would cost $5 for a half hour. Add in the cost of the oil at $5 and, that makes your oil change a $10 expense so far.

Now that you have a pan full of oil, you have to properly dispose of it. So, you must take time to pour your old oil into a proper container so that you can take it to a service station for disposal. Don't forget the oil disposal fee, which is common in most states.

I know, most people illegally dump the oil in their trash or even worse, pour it out in their backyard or into the city drainage system. I am talking to the ethical people who do things legally and properly. If you are going to do it yourself, please, at least do it right! If you do it right, you would add at least another fifteen minutes and an additional $2.50 to $10 to your $10 cost. Now you are up to a cost of between $12.50 and $20. And let's not forget the cost of lost quality time with your family. Have you ever been changing your oil when your son came and asked you to play catch? How do you put a price on that missed opportunity?

Now, I know what you are thinking. "Wait a minute, Mike, what about the thirty minutes I would spend sitting at the oil change store while they change the oil. Isn't that costing me money?" The answer is, it is costing some people money while it is allowing others to make more money. Look around the lobby while you wait. Some people are on cell phones, some are on laptop computers, others are writing proposals, reading contracts, or designing a logo for their small business. They are doing things that will put more money into their pocket, and certainly more than the $5 it is costing them to pay for someone else's time to change the oil. I challenge anyone to not find at least $5 in money-saving coupons and offers that will save you more money on other things, going through the newspaper while waiting for an oil change.

I once pointed out a coupon to a person in the oil change store while we were waiting. It was a coupon for $5 off of an oil change at the very store we were sitting in. She was an elderly woman and her whole demeanor changed once she had that coupon in her hand. She went right up to the counter and proudly presented her coupon and received her discount. You would have thought I handed her a $100 bill, she thanked me so many times.

The key here is to realize that when you hire others to do work for you, it is so you can free up time to increase the quality of your lifestyle, make even more money, or save money. Even if you spend time reviewing and revising your spending plan, you will be getting your money's worth and, more, in the long-run. The old adage "Time is money," is very true and to the point. I suggest you should always be looking for a high rate of return on any time investment you make in anything.

It is a lot of fun to calculate how much money you actually make when you negotiate savings. For example, by taking a minute to ask a salesperson for a lower price and actually getting it, I calculate what amount I earned in that minute. It is a confidence builder that I suggest you use as well. However, it can work the other way also and I try to avoid ever investing too much of my time and money to earn a discount. If it is too much, the discount may not be the bargain it first seemed to be.

WINNING THE SHOPPING GAME

Be sure to give yourself credit for your financial victories when spending money. This will help keep you motivated to continue. Wouldn't it be great if there were audiences at stores who could cheer when you get a great deal? Since that is not the case, we have to be our own cheerleaders knowing we are doing a great job of winning at the shopping game. When you think about it in those terms, just like a professional athlete, at the end of the day you can actually count up your winnings. And, remember, it is what you do with the money you save that really counts over time. You could save a great deal of money today only to spend it all, and more, tomorrow. Building a richer lifestyle starts with smart spending but requires that you also do smart things with the extra income that you generate in the form of savings.

To help you properly manage your surplus from savings, I suggest you record the actual savings to compare against your spending plan's projected savings. You would do this either on your actual spending sheet for the year or on the combined plan/actual spending worksheet. Just as businesses track their income and expenses against their annual budgets, you should also. And be sure to do this as soon as you get home or at your first opportunity so you don't forget. Nowadays savings are printed right on receipts. That makes it easy to create a log of savings or to write directly to your actual spending worksheet. By compiling and tracking this information accurately you can make more intelligent decisions as to what to do with any extra money you have created.

The Perpetual Sale is a good thing for consumers—the smart consumers, or Power Buyers, that is. Readers of this book can consider themselves ahead of the game. Certainly, you will be more sensitive to the "tricks" of the retail trade and my hope is that you will prosper as a result of taking advantage of the many opportunities merchants are giving you to improve your lifestyle at a huge discount.

5

$ $

Everything Is Negotiable

"I can't stress the importance of obtaining as much information as possible on the item for sale and the atmosphere surrounding the sale."

The word negotiation scares many people for some reason. I believe it is the thought of face-to-face confrontation that frightens many. For others it may be personal insecurity or, possibly, the fear of insulting someone. I know I've personally experienced all of these feelings when involved in negotiation, and I don't think I am unusual.

If you are making a conscious effort to avoid situations where you are required to negotiate, or if you simply do not negotiate at all, even if you have the chance, one thing is clear: Failure to negotiate as much as possible is costing you money.

Regardless of what you may think, you negotiate every day; you may not realize that you are doing it, but you negotiate all of the time.

We tend to think of big-ticket items like cars and houses when we think of negotiation, but anyone who has ever traveled outside the United States knows buying something as simple as a Mexican leather belt, for example, can lead to negotiation that would make some international treaty talks look like child's play. In many countries around the world, negotiation between buyers and sellers over every purchase—even for seemingly insignificant things like fruits and vegetables—is part of the culture. Negotiation over price is expected.

Recognizing that most interaction between humans includes some form of negotiation will help you become more successful in life. If you understand that negotiation, just like using coupons, can generate wealth for you and your family, you will find yourself actually looking for chances to negotiate.

With negotiation, in a matter of minutes, you can earn thousands of dollars. Most of us work hours at our jobs in return for dollars. With proper negotiation, you can create dollars in a very short time period. This is called time leverage and it is how people get rich. For example, suppose you are paid $10 an hour at your job. You work one hour and are paid $10 minus taxes. Now, let's say you have just saved $50 in five minutes using negotiation to get a lower price on something. Your salary for that hour would be technically $600 or, $50 earned in five minutes, times twelve. I think you are worth that kind of money. Don't you?

Benjamin Franklin said, "A penny saved is a penny earned." Actually, a penny saved is better than a penny earned because you do not pay tax on that earned income.

I can guarantee you this: As long as you are only paid in direct proportion to your physical time investment, you can never become wealthy. Hourly workers have no way to leverage their time. They work one hour, they get a set wage for that hour. No more, no less. Using all of the principles in this book will allow you to leverage your time as well as generate lots of extra cash flow.

This often-used quote in the tax preparation business works just as well in the business of paying less for everything. "In the end, it is not how much you earn, but how much you keep." There are plenty of millionaires who have spent themselves into bankruptcy. Poor spending techniques are what did them in, not lack of income.

BUILD YOUR NEGOTIATION SKILLS

Obviously, to become good negotiators, we have to understand what good and bad negotiation is. Negotiation, or compromise, happens between people every day. It occurs whether they know it or not. Negotiation occurs when you get up in the morning, on your way to work, at work, at lunch, at home—everywhere. You probably negotiate with yourself more than anyone. For example, when you tell yourself it is all right to eat the bowl of ice cream for dessert because tomorrow you will jog an extra mile, that is negotiation. A win-win situation if I have ever heard of one, as well.

Children are natural negotiators. Have your children ever ignored you when you told them to get ready for bed? That is a form of negotiation. It is a primitive form, but a form nonetheless. They are trying to communicate to you what their position is at the moment, which is, I don't want to do what you want me to do right now. Perhaps you have a teenager who wants to borrow the car. Have you ever noticed how all the chores get done, and even some extras, on the day your child plans to ask you for something? Again, this behavior is a form of negotiation. The children will do something for you in return for something they would like you to do for them. Most people, whether children or adults, have underdeveloped negotiating instincts. Because of this, emotional cues such as tears, pouts, smiles, hugs, an extra "I love you," are often genuine emotions, but also can be used to negotiate a position. And, these unrefined techniques work fairly well. Ask any parent.

Negotiation is communication between two interested parties, which can occur without any verbal communication, as you will soon learn. Some people may think they are good negotiators because they can browbeat anyone into submission. Yelling louder than the other guy does not make you a good negotiator. Tricking someone into doing what you want him or her to do does not make you a good negotiator, either.

Good negotiation allows both sides to win. Yes, you are adversaries in a sense, but there is no rule that says you have to be enemies out to do each other harm. Unfortunately, many people enter negotiations with this attitude and it can lead to frustration. An, "all-or-nothing" attitude in negotiation rarely will allow you to achieve the results you want. Good negotiators are people who realize that a spirit of "give and take" is necessary to ensure success.

Remember, your goal in "purchase negotiation" is to find out exactly how little you can pay for something. You know what the asking price is in most cases; that number simply represents the most you could pay for an item.

A good negotiator is like a detective. The more information you find out in advance (for example, how motivated the seller is), the better your ability to intelligently negotiate a purchase. This is the kind of information you want to find out: How did the seller come up with the asking price? How long has the item been for sale? Why is it for sale? How many are for sale? Is there a chance the asking price may be reduced soon? What have others paid for the same or similar item? Is there a similar item available for less money? Is there a competing store offering the same item?

If you are dealing with an individual selling a house, a car, or another, similar large ticket item, important answers to find out are these: What does the seller intend to do with the cash? How much does he still owe on the item? What have similar items sold for recently?

You should also ask yourself some important questions when entering into a negotiation, as well. For example, "What is the most I am willing to pay for the item? How badly do I want or need the item? Am I willing to walk away from the item if the seller won't sell on my terms?"

Often, what we think is a negotiating point is not material at all. For example, we all naturally assume that price is the primary consideration for both buyer and seller. This is not always the case. If something has sentimental value to the seller, all the money in the world may not be enough to get him to part with it.

Personal feelings can often get in the way of negotiations, creating roadblocks to a successful completion of business. Your personal feelings about the seller, or your first impression of them, can affect your negotiation "attitude." I have found it is always best to avoid judging people on appearance. Remember, the other person's negotiating experience is most likely limited and they may think, like you possibly thought, that good negotiators are tough, hard, and unmovable from their position. So, they are trying to appear as though they will not be pushed around.

Your negotiating posture is very important as well and is dictated by your confidence, or lack thereof. Your confidence is dictated by your knowledge of the buying situation. I can't stress the importance of obtaining as much information as possible on the item being sold and the "selling atmosphere" surrounding the sale. That way, you enter negotiations with some idea of the boundary lines in which you are working.

There are many great books about the topic of negotiation that go much deeper into the subject than I can go here. I suggest you read the classic book by Herb Cohen, *You Can Negotiate Anything*, from Bantam Books. You should also check out Roger Dawson's books, including *Secrets of Power Negotiating*, from Career Books. Reading about negotiating is important to begin to learn basic strategies. But the real way to become a master negotiator is to take the strategies you learn and practice them as much as possible.

TECHNIQUES OF THE TRADE

There are many simple techniques you can use immediately to improve your negotiation results even if you don't have a great deal of experience. Below, we've highlighted several of Roger Dawson's techniques. Many of these techniques will sound familiar to you; they have been used on you many times and you have probably used them yourself either on purpose or by accident.

The Mythical Partner or, Third Party technique is the most commonly used tactic by amateurs who probably don't realize they are negotiating. What they are doing is stalling a buying decision for any number of reasons. I am sure you have used this one, especially if you are married. Statements like, "I need to check with my wife," or "I will ask my husband what he thinks." Businesspeople often use this one with success, "I need to check with my partner [or business associate or boss]."

Other variations on the stall are ones I'm sure you have used, such as, "We are just looking;" or, "We're just browsing."

Whether or not you really have a spouse or a partner in real life, it is usually a good idea to have one when you are in negotiations. Having a third party to refer to allows you to do several things. Stalling for time to think or to find out more information are but two of those things.

The best use of this technique is to take it beyond the stall and see how anxious the salesperson is to sell. For example, say something like this, "I can't make a purchase for that much without consulting my husband." This will prompt the salesperson to ask you at what price you could make a decision. You don't want to give the salesperson a number. Your response should be, "Well, how much lower could you go on the price?" The more anxious the salesperson, the more quickly the answer and the lower the reduction. This also will allow you to ascertain if the person you are dealing with is in a position of authority when it comes to making a deal.

Always negotiate with decision makers. If your salesperson has to go check with someone else to find out if the price can be lowered, you know you need to be dealing with someone else: the individual the salesperson is talking to. This goes on all the time at car dealerships. The salespeople are actually using the third party technique on you. Does this sound familiar: "I have to run that by my manager?" This is usually the truth. Beyond certain strict parameters, lower-level sales representatives don't have the authority to make many decisions, especially to lower price. But, stalling allows them time to plan their next attack on you.

Don't allow this to happen to you. You will be outnumbered and they will win. Besides, your time is very valuable and you don't have time to play games. Insist on speaking to someone who has the authority to make decisions. This is especially true if you are making a major purchase—like a vehicle—for several thousand dollars.

The best time-leverage in negotiating can be gained by getting as close as possible to the actual owner or a direct representative of the owner. Again, attitude is crucial. It is best to explain that you are a serious buyer and you want to work with the owner or sales manager directly. Just be careful not to belittle the sales representatives and they will usually be happy to get someone in charge to help you. As long as their job is not in jeopardy, it is no problem. But the minute you upset the low-level guy, he is going to get the manager and at the same time prepare the manager to talk to you by telling him that you are a problem customer. Now the person in charge is defensive from the start and less willing to give in to any of your demands.

I can tell you from firsthand experience, having worked as the head of sales operations for many years myself, when a customer has a bad attitude, it is often seen as a challenge for the person in charge. All the salespeople are watching how the manager handles this customer. Giving in to a shopper, even on minor points, may appear to be backing down and most sales managers' egos won't allow that.

Some people avoid the real decision makers because it is easy to push low-level sales clerks around. Personally, there is nothing more frustrating than having a clerk bounce between the sales manager and me.

If you want to be right to the point, and you are a serious buyer, ask who is in a position to sell you the item for your price (you pick the amount). For example, if you want to purchase a couch and the asking price is $1,500, you could ask this, "Who is in a position to sell me this couch for $1,000?" This is a sure way to find out who the decision maker is. Be ready to explain why you are only willing to pay $1,000 and you may get a great deal.

Once you identify the decision maker, there are a number of questions you can ask to begin finding out what leeway there is in price and other considerations:

➤ What if I buy today? Have you ever noticed how complacent salespeople get, especially in retail establishments? They are so used to hearing people say, "We're just looking," all day long, that when someone actually says, "I'm ready to buy now," they hardly know how to react, if they react at all. I've actually had clerks say to me, "OK, let me know if I can help you," right after I've said to them, "I'm ready to buy these items."

➤ What if I buy two? If there is a discount for buying two, now you have established that the store is willing to take a lower price on each item. For example, suppose you are looking at a $700 treadmill for your home to help you keep in shape. By asking, you find that the price for buying two of them is $1,300, or, $650 each. You now know that the store is willing to take $650 per treadmill. You have established a lower price parameter.

➤ What if I pay cash? Merchants pay fees of anywhere from 1 to 5 percent of every credit-card purchase to their credit-card processor. By paying cash, you are allowing the merchant to make a bigger profit, not to mention that they get the money today rather than a couple of days later.

Your approach and questioning tactics are controlled somewhat by the nature of what you are attempting to buy. You obviously are in a different situation on a new car lot versus a garage sale, but, the basic premise of negotiation remains. Don't let the fact that you are dealing with an individual selling a personal item change your thinking about your negotiation posture. In fact, you almost always pay a lot less than the original asking price by using these techniques on an individual. They are less experienced in negotiating than businesspeople who do it all day for a living. So, you actually have a better chance of getting more of what you want when dealing with inexperienced individuals.

You don't see a lot of price negotiation taking place in retail stores. People assume that because the price is posted, that must be the final price. However, there are a number of strategies you can use to ensure you don't pay more for something than you have to. Ask yourself and the sales clerk these questions: "If and when is this item going on sale?" "Are there any manufacturer's rebate programs or coupons available?" "Is the store offering any special savings on the item for sale or similar items?" "When is the store's next big sale or inventory clearance, and will this item be included?" "Is there a comparable item available for less?" "Are there any bonuses available if I buy this item?" Bonuses could be things such as free film or batteries when you buy a camera, free CD's when you buy a stereo, a free cell phone when you buy a car.

Have you noticed what it is you are doing when you negotiate? Yes, *asking* questions. *Asking* for discounts. *Asking* for a lower price. *Asking* for bonus items. The secret to getting everything you want in life is simple. *Ask*. Ask and you shall receive. One thing is clear. If you do not ask, you will not get what you want, so never stop asking.

MORE STRATEGIES

There are a few more strategies you should have in your negotiating arsenal.

Re-ask the asking price. Even if the asking price is listed in the ad or on the item, ask what the asking price is. This is especially important if you are calling about a newspaper ad. The seller may have just decided ten minutes earlier to lower the asking price. Ask the seller, "How much are you asking?"

When face to face with the seller, use a wince. (Roger Dawson refers to this technique as "flinching.") You wince by making a sour-looking face. Try to repulse your face and your entire body in disbelief of the asking price. No words are necessary. You are trying to say, without actually saying it, "Are you out of your mind asking that much?" We have all used it subconsciously. Plan to use it consciously every time you ask for a price.

For even more impact, you can add what I call "The Exclamation." For example, if the seller asks a price of $500, wince and then exclaim in a concerned but not necessarily loud voice, "Five hundred dollars?!?" Then, be totally silent and wait for a reaction. Wait as long as it takes for the seller to react. At this point, whoever speaks first loses ground in the negotiation.

The Exclamation works very well over the telephone but complete silence often works better. When someone quotes you a price over the telephone, don't say anything. The silence will signal your disbelief and, often, an individual will react with, "But you can make me an offer," or, "But if you think that is too much you can make me an offer." The door is now open for you to set your price since you now know the seller is willing to take less.

Most individuals trying to sell something have no idea how to price the item. They do not use logic when they choose a price. They most often use sentimental reasoning or guesses to justify the price. "Well, I paid $30 for it three years ago," they may think, "So it has got to be worth at least $25 now." By asking the seller how he came up with the asking price you can often help him realize his asking price is out of line.

This is also a good lesson for you if you are trying to sell something. Ask a price that is consistent with what the market will bear and you will sell the item more quickly. What is very valuable to you may not have that much value to me.

I remember one time when my wife and I had a garage sale and someone offered me 10¢ for one of my favorite high school shirts. I was reluctantly parting with the shirt even though I had not worn it in five years because it didn't fit me anymore.

But, to me that ten-year-old T-shirt was worth a million dollars in sentimental money. "No way," I barked, at the ten-cent offer, and pulled the shirt out of the pile. I haven't worn the shirt since that day, but I was not going to part with my favorite shirt for 10¢, regardless of whether I wear it or not.

The buyer had made the mistake of not finding out enough about the item before throwing out a low-ball price. Had he known the shirt had sentimental value to me, he may have approached the negotiation differently. Even at the ten-cent level, it is important to be a good negotiator in order to get what you want.

Be prepared to walk away. This is perhaps the most important thing you must bring to the negotiation table if you truly want to get the best possible price and terms. If you cannot walk away from the item in question without feeling badly for not getting the item, you have lost the negotiation before you have even started because you will never be willing to push the seller far enough for fear of putting your purchase in jeopardy.

At least, don't let the seller know you love the item and can't live without it. For example, never walk into a house you are considering buying and say something in front of the sellers or their sales agent like, "I love it, it is exactly what we have been looking for." Negotiations are pretty much finished at that point and you will pay the asking price or very close to it. Anytime your opponent knows you cannot walk away, you are at a disadvantage. It is the same disadvantage the seller is at if you know they must sell for some reason.

If you make concessions, get something in return. As I said earlier, good negotiation is a matter of give and take. If you give in on a point, you should ask the seller what he will do for you. You might pay a little more than you planned but get a couple of extras thrown into the deal. Many times, store personnel have more leeway in giving you free merchandise than they do to lower price.

Always negotiate with a smile on your face. Smiling and speaking in a conversational manner will always get you more of what you want. You should avoid showing emotion or reaction of any kind during negotiations, except when wincing. But a smile along with a friendly tone will keep your opponent at ease. The last thing you want to do is put your opponent into a defensive mind-set. An overbearing tone from you can have a negative effect on the person you are dealing with and force them not only to get defensive, but also to feel insulted or belittled, which will certainly put a win-win outcome in doubt.

NEGOTIATING FOR FUN AND PROFIT

In the end, the bottom line of negotiation comes down to supply and demand. The more appealing the item for sale, the less the merchant or individual will be willing to give in to your demands for a lower price.

Understand this fact when going into negotiations, do your homework on the item for sale to the extent possible, and be as confident, yet courteous, as possible during the process, and you will get what you want most of the time.

Yes, to some, the art of negotiation is a game. And, it is true that you can have a great deal of fun negotiating. But it is also a very serious wealth-building tool. As the old saying goes, "Use it or lose it." In all cases, if you don't use negotiation techniques, it will cost you money.

$ $ $ $ $ $ $ $ $ $ $ $ $ $ $ $ **6** $ $ $ $ $ $ $ $ $ $ $ $ $ $ $ $

Travel Like a Millionaire without Spending a Million

". . . the best way to travel for less is to ask more questions."

When you mention travel, most people light up. Traveling to new places, seeing sites you've only read about, and anticipating exciting adventures in romantic locations are what makes travel so popular. We don't only travel for pleasure; business travel is a big piece of the travel business. There are lots of reasons to travel. And, if you enjoy it as much as I do, let me assure you that you can travel more than ever and increase the quality of your trips if you become a smart buyer of travel.

At first glance, travel would seem too expensive for most people, even if they don't plan to travel in high style. The perception is that any travel is expensive, and the cost of good travel is just out of the question. It is true that the cost of travel can be very high. Sometimes it can be outrageously expensive. But, first class travel does not have to be out of reach for you. First class travel can be very affordable, all of the time.

How is this possible? How can it simultaneously be expensive and very affordable for the same quality of travel? The answer is simple: For years, the travel industry, which is ones of the biggest industries in the world, has made its product available at greatly discounted prices. Can you guess why? If your answer is competition, you are right on target. When you start thinking about all the competition in the travel business, it is mind-boggling. From travel agencies to theme parks to cruise ships to hotels to airlines to resorts and campgrounds, it is incredible how many travel options you have from which to choose.

Now, throw in our current economic slowdown and fear of terrorist attacks, and you have a great many companies that are hungry and fighting for your business. These businesses have chosen to compete on price; they have turned their product into a commodity that is sold almost entirely based on the price. Think about it: Did you make your last flight reservations based on the quality of the airplane you'd be flying on and the quality of the service that would be provided by one airline over another? Or, was your decision based totally on the price of the ticket?

THE HIGH COST OF TRAVEL

The travel industry's retail prices are set very high. Not counting the annual family drive back to Dad's hometown and the week's stay at grandma's house, a real vacation—including everything—is not cheap.

The average hotel room in the United States costs close to $100 per night. Airline tickets, ground transportation, tickets to attractions, meals, and miscellaneous expenses can run the average four-member family $1,000 to $3,000 or more for a week, depending on where you go and how you travel. Many families take one big vacation a year. This can be stressful because you want to get your money's worth. Add to that the stress of trying to make everyone in your family happy. It is tough enough renting a movie that will appeal to everyone in your family. Planning one great trip that everyone will enjoy is a thousand times more difficult to pull off—it is your one shot during the year to have a great time.

Using the strategies contained in this chapter, you will learn how to travel more often at half the price or less than you would normally pay. People sitting right next to you on the airplane will be paying double or even triple what you will be paying. Learn and use these techniques and affordable, stress-free, high-quality travel that the entire family enjoys will become a reality for you.

DISCOVERING AIR TRAVEL DISCOUNTS

You will find that in the world of travel, the more questions you ask, the more money you will end up saving. The truth of the matter is most people you talk to when you are planning and buying travel are salespeople, and salespeople are normally paid some sort of sales commission. The more of a discount they give you, the lower their commission will be in most cases. So, unless you ask for a discount or a lower fare, no one is really going to go out of their way to tell you about the discounts that exist. Once in a while, a very helpful travel sales representative will pleasantly surprise you and tell you about every discount available for your trip, but this is rare.

To illustrate this, let me use the airline industry. Most people shop for airline tickets the wrong way. To begin with, they wait until the last minute, which guarantees they will pay more. People usually call two or three airlines and ask how much it will cost to fly to their destination city on a certain day. Airline number one gives them a price and then they call airline number two. They get a price from number two and, maybe call a third, although, finding three major airlines that fly to the same city is getting more and more difficult. Then, they pick the airline that offered the lowest price of the two or three they called.

The problem is, the prices quoted were probably the highest-priced fares available. So, the uninformed traveler is choosing from the two or three highest prices available rather than the lowest available fare. Remember those three words; this is what you should ask for every time you shop for a flight.

If you simply say you want to fly from city A to city B on a certain day at a certain time of day, you limit the responses the salespeople will give you. By asking for the lowest available airfare, they are required to tell you about the fringe flights that are also available, for example, overnight flights, referred to as red-eye flights, and flights leaving very early in the morning.

Airline reservation agents are trained to fill up flights that are lacking in passengers without regard to saving you money. If the noon flight is empty, they are going to try and put you on that flight, even if it costs you an extra $200. Unless you become a good travel detective and dig out the discounts, you'll almost always overpay.

One the most effective techniques for saving money on airline tickets is to plan as far in advance as possible. If you buy airline tickets two or three weeks in advance of a flight you will always save money, and often the savings will be 50 to 60 percent, or more. This goes for cruises and almost every other mode of travel. The early bird gets the savings.

Look at the savings that are available with a little advance research. I discovered this pricing scenario when I researched a flight from Philadelphia to Orlando. A full fare ticket, with no restrictions and no advance purchase requirement, was priced at $838.

The same ticket bought with seven days advance notice was $596, a $242 savings. If we bought the ticket fourteen days in advance, added a Saturday night stay (we couldn't schedule our return flight until Sunday), and some restrictions like non-refundable cancellation (we had to take the trip), non-upgradable (we could not pay to move into first class), the price ranged from $204 to $299. This is a savings of at least $593. Often, you can save 44 to 70 percent simply depending on the month, season, and day of your travel.

If possible, plan to travel during mid-week. The best airline fares are available on Tuesdays, Thursdays, and late nights. In some cities, Saturdays are low fare days. Watch for the seasonal price changes and try to plan your travel for the week right before or after a destination's high season. In the United States, the lowest airfares are available generally between October and March, holidays excluded. If you are flying to Europe, airfares are highest during summer and are lowest from December through March, which is off-season in Europe. Flights to Asia are less expensive from about mid-November through March.

Flexibility is another great asset when it comes to saving travel money. If you can schedule your travel to take advantage of discounts and low fares, you are in a good position to get the lowest prices. The more rigid your schedule, the fewer discounts you will have access to. There is an exception to this rule, however, and it goes back to what I said about managing the occupancy rate. Once a flight is getting close to takeoff and seats remain unsold, those seats may go on the bargain block to the benefit of last-minute flyers. It is difficult to wait to the last minute to try to book a flight if you have to be somewhere at a certain day and time. But, if you are flexible, this can work in your favor.

As a rule, airlines will try to charge you more for flying at the last minute, as if they are doing you a favor for letting you buy a ticket for a seat on one of their airplanes that is still empty. Airlines will make exceptions to the rule of charging more for last-minute travelers in emergency situations or in case of a death in the family. If you truly must travel for some reason, like a family illness or death, and it is a financial hardship for you, be sure to mention this to the agent at the time you make your reservation. I have found airline personnel to actually be very flexible when they can be. They really don't have a problem accommodating you if there is room to do so. They have certain guidelines they have to work within and most are willing to do what they can to help people who are courteous and patient.

I see people blaming the airline service personnel for things out of their control. A lot of frustration comes from the fact that people overpay for airline tickets and then expect to be treated in accordance with how much they paid. Paying more than $300 for a coach ticket anywhere in the United States is not worth it. But, tickets at that price are being sold every day. If you pay $700 and have to fly in the coach section, you will be disappointed and frustrated. My best advice is to avoid ever paying so much for a flight that you feel you have overpaid. Here are some additional ways to cut your travel costs in half without sacrificing quality:

➤ Learn about the discounts available to people less than two years of age and over age sixty-two. Generally, a discount of between 10 and 20 percent is offered to people in these age categories. But, be careful. Don't automatically think the discount is being taken from the lowest available fare. You should find the lowest available fare and then ask for your discount off of that fare. That would be getting a deal.

➤ Opting for a flight with connections rather than a non-stop flight could save you money. This is inconvenient, especially on short flights. If you are traveling with children, the inconvenience of getting off of planes and rushing through airports to make connections may not be worth the savings. If you do choose flights with connections, try to book the earliest possible flights since, as the day goes on, the chance for connecting flights to be delayed or missed increases.

➤ Be sure to book your flights using a credit card that rewards you with membership points. Some credit cards are aimed at frequent travelers and offer a host of benefits like free flight insurance and luggage insurance. If you travel a great deal, it is definitely worth your time to find credit cards that cater to you. Be sure to join the airline's frequent flyer program, even if you don't travel much. Being a member of several of these programs will open a floodgate of discount and promotional travel offers designed to help you travel more.

Researching travel fares and destinations has never been easier thanks to the Internet. Travel Web sites abound with information and savings on everything a traveler needs. One great strategy for using the Internet could end up providing you with an unbelievably low fare and, at least, verify that you have found a good fare. Here is what you can do: Once you have called airlines or researched fares online, take your lowest price and subtract 10 to 25 percent and submit the low price to one of the sites where you name your own price. You may just end up with an incredible deal.

Security concerns are responsible for a new cost that is really becoming an issue and one you should take action to avoid. If you thought your luggage cost a lot when you bought it, wait until you see some of the new fees the airlines are imposing on extra baggage. Some airlines are limiting checked baggage to two pieces per person and charging high fees for each extra bag. Be sure to check on the airline's policies before you show up with extra luggage. Many airlines are also charging extra fees to handle what are considered oversized bags. A bag that measures more than sixty-two inches when you add its height, width and depth is considered by most airlines to be oversized. Fees can be as high as $80 per bag, one way, for domestic travel and several hundred dollars per bag for travel outside of the United States. Traveling lighter will not only save you money, but it can save you time and a great deal of inconvenience as the new security measures require more bag searches.

HOTEL BARGAINS AND DISCOUNTS

Once you get your lowest possible airfare booked, you need to find a place to stay, and one of the easiest places to save money on a trip is at the hotel. Start by asking for promotional specials; group, corporate, and military rates; senior, student, and association discounts; summer, winter, spring, and fall discounts; and off-season discounts. I'm sure you get the point. Ask for discounts!

Spend Your Way to Wealth

There are literally hundreds of discounts available. It may be as simple as paying with a certain credit card to receive a substantial discount. Often, if you fly a certain airline or use a certain rental car company you will qualify for discounts when you stay at a certain hotel chain and vice versa. You have to ask for these things because the salespeople will rarely volunteer this information.

Negotiation plays a major part in hotel savings. If you know of a certain discount offered at a certain hotel, but it is not the one you want to stay at, by mentioning the other hotel's promotion to your desired hotel's reservation agent you might get the same discount at the hotel of your choice.

Again, your ability to bargain is dependent a great deal on availability. If you are traveling to a city with five thousand members of an association you belong to, good luck at the bargaining table. If demand exceeds supply, it is tough to find a cheap rate; conventions usually set up discounted rates for attendees in advance.

Even if the convention facilitator has offered you "discounted" accommodations, shop around anyway. Often, you will find a good rate in a neighboring town away from the action. If the slight inconvenience is not a problem for you, this can be a big money saver. But, if you stay too far away, you may need a rental car, which would add more to your cost than the higher hotel cost for staying at your meeting site.

If you are traveling for pleasure, rather than business, and you do not have to be at a specific location at a specific time, there is another thrifty reason to consider accommodations that are off the beaten path. Hotel tourist taxes, or bed taxes as they are often called, can be as high as 25 percent in some cities. Often, you can save more than half of the tax bill by staying in a nearby city or county. It might be right across the street where the county or city line separates different tax structures, so you may not have to travel far to save big.

One more way to save 10 percent or more on your hotel stay is to know the costs associated with using the telephone in your room, or in the hotel in general. It is frustrating to ponder how out of control these fees have gotten. Even local calls are beginning to get outrageously expensive. The price for convenience is high; hotel telephone usage fees can reach double digits per minute plus tax. You could spend several hundred dollars dialing direct long-distance from the telephone in your room, especially if you are traveling overseas. It used to be that you could dial an outside, local line, then dial the toll-free number on your long-distance calling card and only pay for a local call plus your calling card fees. Now, many hotels are charging you per minute that you are on the local line. (See section below entitled "Phone Home and Save" to learn how to avoid hefty phone charges while on vacation.)

GREAT DEALS AT RESORTS

One of our favorite ways to travel is to stay at condominium resorts. These resorts are a great alternative to hotels, especially for families requiring more than one bedroom. Condos differ slightly from typical luxury resorts in that each condominium is owned by a different owner, whereas in a typical luxury resort, all units are owned by one entity. Each condo is decorated differently, prices are set by the different owners, and amenities vary from condo to condo. If your trip is planned to last more than one or two days, and you are bringing more than two people, including children or teenagers, a condominium resort is not only a financially attractive alternative to a hotel room, but it is also a better choice most of the time when you consider the amenities that are usually included.

Resort personnel often represent the individual owners of the condominiums when they host guests. These owners demand that the guests are well taken care of so they can get return business. They also know that anyone staying at the resort has the potential of becoming a condominium owner, so the management company makes every attempt to provide first-class accommodations. Take a look at these comparisons and you will see why staying at a luxury resort may be your best choice.

With a little shopping around, you should be able to stay at a beautiful condominium resort for a week for between $250 and $500 depending upon season, occupancy rate, and other factors. Of course some will be a bit more expensive but, in general, the price will range between $35 and $71 per night for a seven-day stay.

In a condominium, you can expect to have one, two, or three bedrooms, a living room, a dining room, a fully equipped, eat-in kitchen, washer and dryer, and lots of other comforts of home. A resort will also feature many outdoor amenities on the premises. In addition to the pool, you'll enjoy access to fitness centers, golf courses, and tennis courts. Many resorts will employ social directors who will plan daily activities. Many also have kid's clubs that cater to the needs of children and teens during the day so parents can enjoy some time together to do what they would like to do for a change.

These social directors, or activity coordinators, often have better access to more discounts, special events, and special promotions than the front desk personnel at a hotel. So, you are more likely to be made aware of a few great things to see and do while you are in the area.

Often, your resort stay will include free things like rounds of golf, sightseeing trips at no cost, and transportation to areas of interest for free.

By staying in a hotel, you can expect to pay anywhere from $60 for lower-end accommodations to more than $150 per night. And, as you know, there is no privacy in a hotel room. Certainly there are no kitchen facilities or separate rooms. As the children get older, you may have to have two rooms, which is not only more expensive, but is also a security issue, especially if the rooms don't adjoin with a doorway.

The hotel is perfectly designed to provide sleeping, eating, and meeting accommodations for business people or the traveler who is passing through. I've spent several weeks at a time in a hotel room on business. Though I was comfortable, I still wished that I were staying at a resort. It is simply more like home and I strongly suggest it for any stay of more than a day or two.

There are some all-suite hotels that make the hotel experience a bit more comfortable by creating a separate living area with a fold-out couch and possibly a microwave and small refrigerator, but for a stay of four to seven days, nothing beats resort accommodations.

BURN A WEEK IN THE LAP OF LUXURY

I've mentioned the convenience of condominiums and resorts, and the assortment of amenities available. But did you know that you can stay in the most exotic and luxurious of resorts at rock-bottom prices? You can do this by taking advantage of what the industry calls "burn weeks."

There are thousands of resorts and millions of one-, two-, and three-bedroom luxurious condominiums around the world. For an owner of a resort unit, the worst thing in the world is to have that unit go empty for a week. Someone, either an individual or a resort company, is paying a mortgage and other expenses on that unit.

In many cases, it may not be a time-share type unit. It may be a condominium owned by an individual and leased by a management company on the resort premises. The management company's job is to fill that unit during the times when the owner is not using it.

You can rent these accommodations for as little as $100 for an entire week. I have done it. My family of three (at the time) spent a wonderful week for $100 in an incredible, three-level ski chalet that is built to house ten people. This unit normally leased for more than $1,000 a week. But, the unit was not being used the week we planned to be there; the resort would rather have $100 than nothing. This type of price break on this type of unit is not the norm but there is no telling how much you can save.

We had to wait until the week before our trip to know for sure if we would be able to get the unit, so we had alternative accommodations ready at a much higher price, just in case.

Many travel agents have access to the burn week market. I suggest you call the resort you want to stay at directly and ask if they have any units that are going unused during your planned trip.

Sometimes you will get a great deal of advance notice on a bargain week. More often you will have to wait until shortly before your trip to find out if something is going to be available. When you begin to plan a vacation, contact resorts and ask about their burn-week inventory and other special discounts they might have available.

PHONE HOME AND SAVE

When you travel, it is a good bet that you will be making some telephone calls for a variety of reasons like letting people back home know you are safe. Long-distance calling cards have really become a traveler's best friend in recent years and with the massive changes in the long-distance calling industry, the cost of using a calling card has fallen by as much as 80 percent.

Calling cards can also become a black hole where you throw away lots of money if you are not careful. Here are some basic guidelines for calling cards that should prevent you from paying too much for calls.

First of all, a calling card is cheaper than calling collect. If you call someone collect, you are going to pay many times more than you would with a calling card. Shop for a low-priced calling card, preferably, a card that does not hit you with a surcharge, or "bong" charge, every time you attempt to make a call. This is a fee that is charged for each call you make, usually 25¢ to $2, on top of the long-distance cost, per minute of usage. You can easily find a calling card with no surcharge.

Next, shop the price-per-minute charge. This is an amount that you pay for each minute you are speaking. If you don't pay more than 18¢ per minute with a calling card you are doing well. If you are paying more than 18¢ per minute, and paying a surcharge, you are paying too much. Find another card or tell your current provider you need a more affordable pricing plan.

If you are traveling out of the country, make sure your calling card has international calling capabilities. Don't assume it does. If you travel outside the country a great deal, then you want to check into a service called "international call-back."

International call-back, which is becoming more widely available as the technology allows it to do so, will offer you huge savings on international calls. Here is how it works: You place a call from London, for example, to New York. You have an international call-back service in place, the call is connected in New York, terminated, and then you are immediately called back at the location in London where you made the call.

You see, it is cheaper to call London from New York than it is to call New York from London. That may change in the next ten years as the telephone companies work on connecting the telephone systems of the world together, which should further reduce rates. This service offers major savings for companies with offices in cities around the world but could also benefit you if you travel abroad often.

Beware of credit cards that also offer you calling-card privileges. You will often pay much higher prices for calls in order for the credit card company, or whoever is marketing the long-distance service, to earn commissions.

Make sure your pin number, which is a pass code you are required to dial in order to complete your card call, is not printed on the card itself. If it is and you lose the card, or it is stolen, someone else will be able to use your card and you will get the bill.

Also, as a safety precaution, be careful to cover the dial pad when you dial your access numbers at a phone booth, especially at airports where thieves specialize in stealing your calling card numbers and reselling them.

If the only reason for using your calling card is to place calls to one location, like home or the office when you are away, I suggest you look into getting a toll-free number to use instead. That way you don't have to worry about losing a calling card or dialing in lots of access numbers. Again, if you are traveling outside the country, be sure your toll-free number has international capabilities.

A toll-free number for your home won't cost more than $5 per month and should be as cheap per minute as a regular long-distance call at no more than 4 to 5¢ per minute. Not even the incredibly popular and convenient cellular telephone service can beat that price per minute.

Pre-paid calling cards are another great way to both save money and control the cost of long-distance calling. Commonly used in Europe and other parts of the world for many years, pre-paid calling cards have only recently caught on in the United States.

As the name implies, you pre-pay for a certain amount of talk time, an hour for example. When you are ready to make a call, you dial some access numbers and you are connected. At the beginning of each call, a recording will inform you of how much talk time you have left. When you have used all of the talk time, more time can be added to the card. This is called re-charging the card and can be done by calling the company that issued the card and adding more time and paying for it with a credit card. Or, the calling card can simply be thrown away.

There are many benefits to the pre-paid calling card if you can find a good price. A good price per minute would be no more than 10¢ per minute with no access charge. Watch out for access or connection fees that can be as high as $3 for each call that you make. That money comes right out of your allotted time on the card. The connection fee is charged as soon as you connect even if you connect with an answering machine, voice mail, pager, or wrong number.

You must calculate the per-minute charge at the time you buy the card. Just divide the cost of the card by how many minutes of talk time you are purchasing. For example, if you buy a one-hour (sixty minutes of talk time) card for $15, you'd be paying 25¢ per minute ($15/60 minutes = 25¢). However, the connection fees per call must also be calculated into your ultimate cost per minute. Look for these fees either printed on the card or posted where you purchase the card. If you are not sure what fees you will pay, generally there will be a toll-free number on the card where you can call to recharge it. Call and ask for a listing of usage fees. Watch out for the access fees on pay phones also. These fees are federally mandated in this country and also eat into your calling card's allotted value. The billing increments of your card are important to know also; the lower increments the better. For example, six-second billing increments are better than three minute increments, meaning that, even if you talk for only one minute, you will be charged for using three minutes. Sometimes even six-second billing increments are still rounded to the next minute. It pays to read the fine print.

If you lose a pre-paid card or if a thief steals the access codes from you your liability is limited to the amount of time already on the card. The thief won't be able to exceed the pre-paid call time, unless he also has your credit cards.

Businesses like the pre-paid card because it allows them to have more control on costs. By pre-paying, a company can decide in advance how much it wants to spend on long-distance.

Parents with children away at college or on other school or vacation trips find this technique valuable as well. First-year college students tend to get lonely and call home a lot. They also make friends from all over the world and like to keep in touch with them, on the telephone. They will occasionally let a friend use their card. If your child has access to a regular, unlimited, long-distance calling card, you run the risk of getting a surprise in the mail in the form of a huge long-distance bill.

With pre-paid calling cards, parents can decide how much they are willing to spend each month for long-distance and then recharge the card for a certain number of minutes. Once those are used, the student can add more time herself or simply wait until next month for you to refill the card. Many parents report that this is just one technique they use to teach their children the value of money.

Cheap cellular telephone costs are allowing cell phones to quickly take over as the communication tool of choice for everyone, especially travelers. If you are going to rely on your cellular telephone when you travel, be sure to check with your provider before you leave to make sure you will have uninterrupted service in the areas you will be visiting. Often, some simple programming is required before you leave your home city in order to get service in your destination city. I once spent a month in California without cellular service because I did not perform a simple programming task on my telephone before I left, so the California provider could not recognize my telephone as being part of its system.

Also, check the costs of using your cellular telephone in the cities where you will be traveling. Roaming fees can sometimes make the cost of using your cellular telephone very expensive. Ah, the high price of convenience.

For safety during car trips of any length, cellular phones cannot be beat. Don't forget to bring extra batteries or your charger.

SAVING ON CAR RENTALS

Back on the road, literally, let's talk about winning the car rental game. All of the rules that apply for booking airline tickets are valid for renting vehicles. Advance reservations are the key to saving money. If you book your rental seven to fourteen days in advance, you will almost always receive discounted rates. If you show up at the car rental counter unannounced, anywhere in the world, be prepared to pay top dollar. If you must rent a car at the last minute like that, you are advised to pass up the big, well-known companies, and seek out smaller, local companies with locations away from the airport. You generally always save money by picking your rental car up off the airport's property, even if you rent from the name-brand companies.

Again, the Internet gives you incredible research power when it comes to shopping rates for rentals. Ask for discounts and special promotional offers. Memberships that you have in different organizations may provide a discount or you may qualify for a senior discount. Remember, the quoted price will usually not include taxes, location fees, insurance, second driver fees, drop-off charges, and other extras that can add 10 to 30 percent to your cost.

Always choose to return the rental car with a full tank of gas. It may be inconvenient but you will save a lot of money. The rental company will charge you a very high, premium price per gallon, plus additional sales tax and airport fees could also be tacked on to the bill.

Another task often overlooked in our zeal to get going after a long flight is the inspection of the vehicle. Go over the car very carefully before you take possession and note any existing damage carefully. It may seem inconvenient, but you will be glad you caught the dent in the bumper before you drive off because the rental company will catch it when you return the car and the repair will not be cheap.

Finally, be sure to ask your airline and hotel if they have any special money-saving, promotional programs with any car rental companies.

ADVANTAGES OF THE MINI-VACATION

There has been a real trend growing over the past few years for people taking short two-, three-, and four-day trips, as opposed to full one- and two-week vacations. This is mostly due to the fact that, though our leisure time is supposed to have increased, people work too much to even consider taking a week or two off at a time. Many are afraid to be away from the office for too long, especially in a difficult economic environment, which accounts for continuing downsizing. It is a shame that so many employees fear being perceived as expendable. But, who can blame them, especially after what has happened in the last year?

Actually, taking shorter trips, but more of them, is a great way to recharge the batteries. Longer vacations can actually make you weary, which is the opposite of what you were trying to accomplish. Also, with longer trips, we tend to go to the big destination, bypassing the great local spots that weekend trips allow us to enjoy. Think about how many great places and things there are to see and do that are just a car ride away. There may be places you don't even know about within a few hours from where you live that would make fabulous mini-vacation spots.

If there are resorts or attractions located within driving distance or a short flight from where you live that you would like to visit, perhaps more than once a year, contact them and ask about any discount offers or savings programs they may offer frequent visitors. Many cities and towns offer local residents, or people from the same state, a discount.

It is very common to save a great deal of money and enjoy your travel more if you travel and stay off of the beaten path. Independent inns, hotels, and bed and breakfasts in smaller towns can give you a more realistic feel for the area you are visiting. Don't be afraid to venture off of the interstate highways. Travel should always be an adventure.

WORK WITH A TRAVEL AGENT—OR BECOME ONE

If all of this research and negotiation seems like it will be too much for you, you might consider using the services of a travel agent or travel consolidation company. Many people don't use travel agents because they are not quite sure how those agents make their money. The truth is that travel agents still make most of their money in the form of commissions from the airlines, hotels, cruise lines, and car rental agencies. There was a time when it cost the traveler nothing to use the travel agency's service. But, that is changing now that the airlines and other travel vendors have drastically cut commissions they pay to travel agents. Airlines and others are opting to sell their product online. Displacing the human workforce is one of the ill effects of the growth of the Internet. In many respects, the Internet, with its vast amount of information and fast search capabilities, has taken the place of the travel agent.

A good travel agent can be very helpful in organizing your travel plans and doing research. Individuals should consider using a travel agent for special trips. For example, some inside knowledge will be very helpful if you take a cruise or a trip to some exotic location or foreign country that you've never been. It is my experience that you can do just as well on your own for basic, domestic travel planning that consists of little more than airfare, hotel, and a rental car.

Remember, travel agents are salespeople paid on commission. The more you pay for the trip, the higher the commission the agent will earn. There may also be financial incentives offered to agents if they use certain vendors, regardless of your particular financial needs. So, it is not in their best interest to push too many discounted fares your way. Even though you don't technically pay the commissions to the agents, you actually do by paying higher travel prices.

As with anything, you have to be an informed consumer. Leaving every detail in the hands of professional salespeople leaves you at risk of paying more than you have to. If you decide to use a travel agent, call some agents in the city where you are planning to travel. Since these agents will be much more familiar with what is going on in their city, they may have access to information or special pricing, which your local agent may not be aware of.

Here is a great strategy if you really love to travel and like the idea of making money while doing something you enjoy. Consider going into business as a home-based travel agent. There are some good, legitimate programs out there that allow you to start your own travel business for less than $400. These business-opportunity companies provide training, credentials, and give you access to real travel agencies so you can earn referral fees and commissions when clients book travel through you. Sometimes these programs are offered directly by travel agencies.

One of the major benefits to being in the travel business is the opportunity to earn what are known in the business as FAM trips. (FAM is short for familiarization.) Resort owners and other travel wholesalers and retailers know that the more familiar you are with a destination, the more apt you are to recommend it to your travel clients. So, if you are selling travel legitimately, you will often have the opportunity to visit great destinations very inexpensively and often for free.

As a home-based travel agent you will have the opportunity to earn credentials that identify you to others in the industry. This identification can allow you to receive special discounts on all types of travel as well as free and low-cost FAM trips if you are really selling travel to people other than yourself. Not to mention all of the benefits of owning your own small business.

However, due to abuse by people masquerading as travel agents simply to save money, and unscrupulous business people selling travel agent IDs, the travel industry has tightened up in regard to who gets access to travel agent discounts. So you may be scrutinized a bit more these days than in the past. If you have earned legitimate credentials and are honestly trying to do some travel business, you have nothing to worry about.

If you do consider getting into the travel business and decide to enroll with a company offering a home-based travel business, be careful to deal only with companies that are actually operating real travel agencies or at least have solid connections to established travel agencies. I suggest you contact the travel agency through which you will be ultimately booking travel and verify everything about the program. Visit the agency in person if at all possible and check with the state that the agency is based in to make sure the company has the proper licensing. Also, verify that the travel agency is a member in good standing of organizations such as the International Airlines Travel Agent Network (IATAN), Cruise Line International Association (CLIA), and the American Society of Travel Agents (ASTA). There are no federal licensing requirements for travel agents. Nine states require some form of registration or certification of retail sellers of travel. As a home-based business, your state and local governments may require you to have a business license. The agency should also be accredited by the Airline Reporting Corporation (ARC), and the International Air Transport Association (IATA). As with any business opportunity, check the company out completely before investing any money. And do not just get into the business to save money; there are plenty of travel savings clubs you could join for a lot less than the cost of starting a home-based business.

CRUISING LIKE A MILLIONAIRE

You can travel like a millionaire in other ways as well. Cruising is wonderful! Amazingly, a very small portion of the population has actually been on a cruise. However, year after year, cruise companies keep forecasting huge demand for their product, which causes the construction of new cruise ships. With such great supply and little demand, discounts can be had at 50 percent or more off of the retail price of cruises.

Because of the high cost of building cruise ships, like airplanes, these ships tend to remain in use for a very long time. That is why one of my biggest pieces of advice to you is to check out the cruise line thoroughly and ask for actual pictures of the cabin you will be staying in during your cruise.

Never assume you will be staying in a luxury suite like those you saw on the television show *The Love Boat*. Remember, that was TV. In reality, depending on how much you spend for your shipboard accommodations, you could end up in a cabin that is twenty years old with bunk beds and extremely small bath and dressing areas. Keep in mind, even though cruise ships are huge, it is still a boat, not a resort or hotel, so there is limited space to begin with. Some ships, on the other hand, are very luxurious. They also cost much more. The best way to avoid any surprises when you get to the ship is to do your homework, even if you are booking a trip on one of the more popular cruise lines.

The ports of call are also very important when choosing a cruise. That is where you will spend your days, and often some nights, and you should make sure there are activities available for everyone in the family, especially the kids. Cruise lines are attempting to become "child-friendly" with the addition of children's activities but I suggest you check on what night-time activities, if any, are available. This is crucial if you and your spouse plan to enjoy some of the entertainment and gambling facilities aboard the ship after dinner. Most of the shows take place in bars, and the gambling is certainly not suitable for minors, either. There is usually a movie theater that may or may not be showing a family movie. Be sure to ask for a schedule of movies to be shown in advance.

Some cruise lines offer babysitting and childcare. Get a schedule in advance so you can plan your vacation just as you would at any other destination.

Here is a quick cruise tip that the cruise lines will hate me for giving out. But my allegiance has to be to you, my loyal reader. On board the ship, the cruise line will offer to sell you tickets to many things such as scuba diving trips, gambling junkets, sightseeing trips, and more. Pressure is put on you to purchase these items before the ship docks at the port.

Most of the time, you can save money by purchasing these items off the ship once you get into town. You can actually negotiate better prices on shore, by dealing directly with the providers, as you won't be paying extra to cover the cruise line's commission.

But, as with anything you buy, be careful to deal with legitimate businesses. Ask for identification. A receipt tells a great deal about who you are dealing with. Illegitimate operators rarely give receipts with business addresses and telephone numbers imprinted on them and they usually demand cash only.

Keep in mind that when you travel to distant lands, the locally accepted way of doing business may not be exactly like what we are accustomed to here in the United States. Many times salespeople meet you as you leave the boat and will offer you a wide variety of discounts. Not all of them are going to be working for real travel companies. Some may be working for themselves and may not have all of the trappings of a "legitimate" business, but could still provide wonderful service.

I am reminded of one cruise my wife Lori and my son Drew, who was two years old at the time, took to the Bahamas. We thought it would be great to go on a snorkeling trip and waited to get off the ship before purchasing the outing.

Upon leaving the ship we took a taxi ride to a town square and were directed to the beach where we found a gentleman selling snorkeling trips for less than half of what was being charged aboard the cruise ship. The salesman was in an official looking uniform and had legitimate looking receipts. The snorkeling boat was about to leave for the half-day adventure so we went for it.

It was definitely an independent group hosting this trip aboard what seemed to be a very old—if rust is any indicator—and often-used vessel without a lot of luxury seating. But, hey, we were there to snorkel and, besides, we just got off of a luxury liner. The trip called for a ride of about two miles out to sea where we would then snorkel.

I suppose we were about a quarter mile away from the dock when I began to fear what could happen if these gentlemen were not legitimate. Here I was with my two-year-old on an old boat in a foreign country on our way out to sea with a camera and money and feeling very vulnerable. I thought the worst. But, we were on the boat with several other people from our cruise, which was comforting. Nevertheless, the thought did cross my mind that I had jeopardized the safety of my family to save some money.

Once we started snorkeling and enjoying the beautiful underwater scenery, my feelings of anxiety were gone. The crew couldn't have been more friendly and courteous. They made a special effort to entertain Drew by spearing some fish and bringing them aboard, to his delight.

That snorkeling adventure and the pictures we took of it are some of my favorite travel memories. I can't imagine if we had missed it. And, to make it even better, we saved a great deal of money.

Fall is bargain time to cruise the Caribbean. June through August is high-season and will be more expensive. The most expensive time to cruise is Christmas and New Years.

If you do not live within driving distance to the port from which your cruise ship will be leaving, and most people in the United States do not live that close to a port, you will be required to fly or drive to the port city. This is a good reason to utilize a travel agent, who often can put together an attractive cruise package that includes the airline and possibly a hotel stay in the port city either before or after the cruise. Don't forget that taxes and port charges will always be added onto whatever prices you are quoted for a cruise.

TAKING ADVANTAGE OF FREE VACATION OFFERS

Have you ever received a travel certificate in the mail? These are those official-looking certificates that arrive in the mail announcing that you have won a vacation. In order to receive your vacation you need to place a call to the company's office where you will then speak to a tele-sales person who will attempt to sell you a vacation.

These programs aren't all bad, but don't be fooled by any promise of a free vacation. You will need to pay something. And do not call any 900 numbers to find out if you are an instant winner of a fabulous trip for the whole family. That is simply a ploy to get you to call the 900 number, which will cost you money to find out you did not win.

But, there are many, legitimate travel marketing companies offering good, discounted trips if you agree to stay at a certain resort. Some require you to agree to attend a time-share sales presentation in order to get the discounted trip. We will talk about time-share shortly.

The fine print is very important on these offers that come in the mail. Read the offer several times very carefully. Then have two or three other people in your family read it to catch anything you missed.

If you are the type who is easily persuaded to make impulse-buying decisions, do not call for information. Let someone else with a stronger will make the call for you. Ask the company to send you information like pictures of the resort, and details of the trip and prices in writing.

Don't let high pressure tactics such as, "You must make a decision today or you will miss out," cause you to make an expensive mistake. Check the company out thoroughly before you authorize any purchase. Call your state's attorney general's office and ask if they have had any complaints on the company. Check with your local postmaster if you receive an offer in the mail and ask about any problems with fulfilling the products offered.

In most states, organizations that sell or market travel are required to be registered. Request the business's state license number and ask the salesperson how long the company has been in business, where the office is located, and for a local telephone number where you can call back. Hesitation in answering these types of questions signals either a very new salesperson or an illegitimate company. Ask if the company is listed with the chamber of commerce or Better Business Bureau.

Be sure to write down the exact details of the trip the company is selling. You will need this information so you can shop the same trip on your own to see if you are truly getting a bargain.

When you decide it is safe to proceed further with the company and you are given a price for the trip it is selling, negotiate with the salespeople. Ask them if that is the best they can do. For more on negotiating, refer to chapter 5 for tactics and strategies that will save you money. Beware of companies that demand you send cash only. This is a sign that the company is attempting to do business without any paper trails like cashed checks or credit card statements. Legitimate operators will normally take credit cards, checks, and money orders.

TO TIME-SHARE OR NOT TO TIME-SHARE?

As I say, most free travel offers are a way to get you to attend some sort of time-share sales presentation. The topic of time-sharing could be a book subject unto itself. Also known as Interval Ownership, buyers purchase ownership in resort accommodations for seven-day stays. These are known as time-share weeks. You purchase a week of the year during which you have access to the accommodations. The initial investment can be from $5,000 to $30,000, which most people finance. You will also have to pay annual maintenance fees, which can average $300 to $500 per year. It is really hard to justify investing that much money in buying and maintaining time-share accommodations unless you have a really good reason.

Many people buy a week with the idea of trading for stays at different resorts each year. Yes, in many cases, you can trade weeks at other resorts if weeks are available at a resort where you want to go. Be sure to read the fine print of your contract and get a list of fees that will be required to trade weeks. This process can be time-consuming and costly, depending on where you want to go. The more popular the resort, the tougher it will be for you to get a week there.

In my opinion, you need to decide if the money invested on an annual basis in the mortgage and maintenance of the time-share accommodations would not be better off invested properly and growing for you in some other financial instrument.

If you are thinking it will be an investment that will grow in value, reconsider. The time-share re-sale market is tough because there are so many bargain basement repossessions for sale and owners who want out of their commitment that it would be difficult for you to recoup a large investment.

In fact, the place to buy a time-share is on the secondary market. If you want to buy a week, look in the paper for owners who are motivated to sell their investment. You can often buy weeks for a third of what the original owner paid. He may only owe a couple thousand dollars on the week but doesn't have the time to travel or is tired of paying the annual maintenance fee.

The question to ask yourself is why are you considering time-share. If it is to save money, you may be mistaken. Certainly you can buy a trip for the same or less than the cost of the annual maintenance and mortgage payments.

AND DON'T FORGET THE COUPONS!

There are so many ways to save money when you travel and so many places to find bargains, discounts, special promotions, and freebies that it is impossible to include everything in one chapter. My newsletter dedicates an entire section monthly to the subject of travel and will continue to be a great source of up-to-the-minute travel savings information.

An often overlooked way to save money is to request coupons in advance. For example, one year as we planned a skiing trip to Park City, Utah (one of my favorite destinations in the entire world, by the way), we asked each travel company we spoke with, like the rental car company, if any discounts or special promotional offers were available in addition to the discount we were getting on the car rental. The clerk told us of a special winter promotional package that he would send to us. Just a few days later, we received much more than we had hoped for in the mail. In fact, a large discount book full of money-saving coupons and discount offers was sent in addition to a complimentary membership in a National Ski Association, which gave us access to many additional discounts and services. This package became an invaluable companion during our trip and the savings allowed us to enjoy twice as much as our initial budget had room for. We learned about many great local shops and attractions that we might have missed without this package.

Always ask the hotel or resort you plan to stay at, as well as the airline you'll be flying, and any other travel vendor you come in contact with while planning your trip, about money-saving offers and promotional programs that might be available. If they don't have any available, often they can tell you who does.

Manufacturers of products are a good source of money-saving programs especially if they create and sell specialty items for special seasons. If you are planning a ski trip and need to buy snow boots, check for special offers like free ski lift passes with the purchase of a company's boots.

Once you get to your destination, begin looking for visitor coupon books, magazines, and other publications when you visit stores and restaurants. Hotel lobbies and rooms are other great places to look for these publications. Don't forget to check the phone book. In most cities the phone book will include money-saving coupons.

Travel magazines are full of discount offers and news about special events in cities around the world. When looking for magazines, be sure to look for copies of the local paper from the city you plan to visit. It will be full of information on local events and certainly will be full of money-saving coupons.

Hopefully, you can see the value of planning travel in advance and asking many questions. All of your research can be done using a telephone and a computer in just a few hours time. Getting information in advance of a trip and using it to your advantage is the key to traveling first class for less. Once you arrive at your destination, your main goal should be to have a good time.

7

$ $

Buy the Car of Your Dreams at Half Price

"There is too much anxiety surrounding the purchase of a car. It is like walking into a den of lions. You know you have no chance. Or do you?"

You will spend a great deal of time and money preparing to purchase, negotiating a purchase, and ultimately, paying for the purchase of vehicles during your lifetime. The average person will own, or should I say, make payments on, at least seven vehicles during his or her lifetime. If you have children who will eventually become teenagers and need a car, you will be involved in extra car purchase transactions that will make an already challenging task much more difficult. Finding a car that is cool enough for a teenager to be happy driving, and also finding one that is affordable, is a remarkable undertaking in and of itself. Forget about the formidable task of dealing with the people who will be selling and financing that vehicle.

The car buying process has been written about quite a bit in recent years. The many dealer tactics for extracting every possible penny of profit out of every vehicle sale have been well documented and exposed to consumers. The fact that these sometimes tricky (and always profitable for the dealer) techniques have been exposed to the public has led, in my opinion, to a great increase in the stress and anxiety surrounding the purchase of a vehicle. Like they say, "What you don't know can't hurt you." This is true, in part, when it comes to buying a car. When we did not know so much about how the dealers and manufacturers were gouging us at every turn, we weren't as anxious about stepping onto the dealer's lot. Now that we know more about the strategies used to sell cars, which start from the minute we read an advertisement in the paper, or hear one of those loud car commercials on the radio, and continue right through to the financing department and the service department, it makes the entire event very stressful, and one we wish we could avoid. It is a bit like the difference between knowing you are walking through a field full of dangerous land mines and taking the same walk but not knowing there are any mines in the field. Once you know the danger exists, your stress level goes way up as you work hard to avoid being hurt by things you cannot see.

To my knowledge, unlike walking through fields full of landmines, no person has ever died as a result of shopping for a car. I can't say for sure, but I don't think the experience is quite as dangerous physically as walking through a minefield. However, it is an experience that can be very dangerous to your financial plan. If you make mistakes, it can cause the ruin of your long-term financial goals and good credit standing. And I know plenty of people who have gotten very ill during and after the car shopping experience. Myself included. This is especially true once you realize how bad a deal you may have signed up for. It is such an exhausting experience for most people; they don't even read the paperwork and the fine print on the contract until after they get home from several hours at the dealership. Many people never read their contract. I've heard people in a dealership say, "I don't care what the paperwork says, just tell me my monthly payment and let me go home."

I do feel, however, that we would stand to be hurt much worse financially by not knowing as much as we now know about the entire car selling system. In this sense, what we don't know *can* hurt us because it puts us at the mercy of a very powerful, well-oiled—pardon the pun—selling machine.

WHY TAKE A CAR LOAN?

Most people finance vehicle purchases for five years. How can you blame anyone? The average sticker price for a new vehicle is more than $21,000. Few people have that kind of cash available to use for buying a new car. And, admit it, even if you had that much cash in your savings account, would you really consider taking it all out and using it to buy a car? Probably not. We have been programmed over the years to pay for large purchases by financing them and paying for them on a monthly basis. Who do you think has done this programming? Yes, the banks and finance companies. It is how they stay in business and make their profits. Big profits, I might add. The consumer's reliance on financing big purchases also allows companies that sell very expensive items, like car dealers, to keep increasing their prices. This has led to amazing growth in the cost of vehicles over the years.

At the same time, we are told to do everything possible to build up savings for retirement, college tuition, and emergencies. This is confusing and makes it difficult for the average consumer to mentally justify parting with over $20,000 in cash to buy a car. Even if it made sense financially to pay cash, it would be a difficult decision for the average person. This is a very important point I would like you to understand. It is generally a good idea to avoid paying interest when you buy anything. However, when you take into account the prevailing interest rates for car loans and rates of return on investments you could be making, it may not make financial sense for you to pay cash for a car or any other large purchase just to avoid the interest cost, even if you can afford to pay the cost of the item in full. Since we are constantly managing many different interest rates and payments for our families, such as credit cards, automobile purchases or leases, mortgage interest, and the interest on other types of loans, we must be selective and smart about what interest we choose to carry on our debt load. It can be a difficult decision, but, a very important one that will change with time. As the prime interest rate keeps getting lower and the price of borrowing money gets cheaper, a car loan's interest rate may be very reasonable when compared with credit-card interest rates that you may be carrying. If you have an 18 percent interest rate on an $8,000 credit card debt, financing your car at 5 or 6 percent interest and putting extra cash on the higher credit card debt makes the most sense. Paying cash for a car you could finance at 6 percent but continuing to pay the minimum payment on an 18-percent interest-rate credit card is a bad decision. By the way, if I were in that situation, I personally would seek to pay off the credit card before I even thought about buying or leasing a car. However, I live in the real world and realize you don't always have a choice. If your car stops running, or is costing you more each month than a new car would cost to keep running, it is a requirement to get some wheels that run no matter how much debt you have. You have got to get to work or nobody gets paid.

At the end of the day, it is usually a good idea to avoid paying interest on a depreciating item like an automobile. This is the biggest problem with buying a vehicle. They begin to depreciate in value from the minute you drive them off of the dealer's lot. In reality, they are depreciating every minute they sit on the lot as well. Unlike a house, which can appreciate in value as it ages because of location and other factors, cars lose value as they age. Except for very rare vehicles and collector's items, the average car or truck loses 50 to 60 percent of its value in the first two years after it rolls off of the assembly line.

It is difficult to win financially when you buy a vehicle. It is an expense, not an investment. But, you have no choice. Our society demands mobility. As our cities become more spread out, it just isn't practical for anyone to think they can do without a car. If you have ever used public transportation you know that it is not something you want to rely on for all of your transportation needs.

DEALING WITH THE DEALERS

So, we are left with the realization that we must deal with the sellers of automobiles. Again, we are operating in a system that requires us to spend money to survive. In the case of automobiles, we have to spend a lot of money. But, you can still spend your way to wealth in the area of car buying. There are few areas of personal finance where it is so important and can be so profitable over the long-term to be a Power Buyer.

Most people settle for the cheapest car they can find that may still meet their family's needs. I am here to tell you that you don't have to settle for a vehicle that you don't like simply because of price. You can drive better cars for the rest of your life by arming yourself with some powerful knowledge and proven strategies.

If you want to get a good deal on a new car, I think you first have to define for yourself what a good deal is. Unlike the real estate market, it is extremely difficult, if not impossible, to find undervalued vehicles for sale. Car dealers have huge overhead costs in order to be in the business, from staff to inventory to advertising, and therefore must mark up their product accordingly. Dealers also have the opportunity to include add-on costs and fees and we really don't have much of a choice but to pay them. Even though there are many car dealerships in most cities now, there are still a limited number of them. And they all play the same pricing and sales games so it does not matter where you go. If you don't like dealership number one you can certainly go to dealership number two. But, dealership two won't be much better. Don't forget that the dealers are also in the financing business. This gives them added leverage to create a profit due to our lack of knowledge.

You have a better chance of finding a good deal from an individual owner selling a car. However, individual owners who have their cars for sale are either having trouble making their own payments and owe more than the car is worth, or they are selling a very old car. Whether you deal with an individual or a dealership, you are going to have to be a tough and knowledgeable negotiator in order to save money and avoid being stuck with high payments over a long period of time.

You won't be able to define your good deal until you do some pre-negotiation research. Only through detailed research will you know how much is too much to pay in all areas of the vehicle purchase. This includes standard equipment, add-ons, financing, extended warranties, and any other item that could be included in the transaction. You cannot fake this. The professional salespeople know when you are faking. They have a product you want and they know it. Your goal is to learn the language of car sales and financing. Once you get your bearings—like speaking the language in a foreign country—you will be able to get around much more easily and you won't be easy prey for sales tactics and often confusing negotiations.

A popular strategy is to simply never buy a new car. If you buy vehicles that are two to three years old, you will have the opportunity to save money. It is not automatic, however. Since car dealers realize that savvy consumers are onto the depreciation of new cars, they have had to refine their tactics in the used car market as well. Used cars offer car dealers equal opportunity to mark vehicles up beyond their market value. There are plenty of unsuspecting used car shoppers. This is especially true among people who have had past financial problems, which may have damaged their credit. With damaged credit, it is more difficult to qualify for the lowest interest rates, so these consumers have little choice but to shop for less-expensive used cars. If you need a car and have little time to shop, have damaged credit, and are uninformed about the basics of smart car buying, the worst place for you to be is on a dealer's lot. You have little to no chance of leaving the lot in a positive financial position.

I think it is a good time for me to make the point that I do not think car dealers and automobile manufacturers are bad people. Just the opposite, they are some of the sharpest business minds in the world. They have mastered their business like few entrepreneurs have. You must respect that. Yes, there are bad operators in every industry who will taint everyone in that particular business by their unethical behavior. The business of automobile sales lends itself a bit more easily to anti-consumer behavior, so those in this, business have gotten a great deal of bad press over the years. In the end, you have to deal with this group, so you can choose to lose, or plan to win. It is totally up to you.

While you are doing your homework, it also makes sense to fully research the complaint records of car dealers you may choose to visit with your state or local consumer protection agency or Better Business Bureau before you spend a great deal of time on the lot.

As I have said, information and knowledge are the keys to winning the car-buying game. But, even before you start shopping and researching, you have got to take a serious look at your family's financial position and what your family needs for proper and safe transportation.

HOW MUCH CAR CAN YOU AFFORD?

You must decide in your spending plan exactly how much you can afford to pay for a vehicle on a monthly basis and, also, in total. You also need to plan how much of a down payment you can make. A car dealer is going to try to qualify you for the most expensive car possible, as you would expect. You must choose a car that will fit into your plan. Again, this purchase is a pure expense. Emotion should not factor into the business decision. If you want a more expensive car, you need to know what it costs new and used. You need to then plan your spending around your desire for that type of car. You can save 10 to 20 percent on the new vehicle you want by doing research and learning to be a good negotiator. You can save 50 percent or more by buying the car you want used. If you want a new car, there is no way you will ever purchase the vehicle for 50 percent off of the purchase price. Not even the dealers can get new cars at 50 percent off of the manufacturers suggested retail price.

The first thing to do is to decide on a class of vehicle that best fits your lifestyle. How will the car be used? If you're concerned about taking your kids to football and soccer practice, you're probably going to need a car with lots of seating and storage capacity. If you're planning to use the car for commuting long distances to work, gas mileage and comfort may be your biggest considerations.

Next, decide what features you simply must have. You have lots of choices for comfort like air conditioning, lumbar supports, anti-lock brake systems, integrated seat belt systems, head injury protection, and child protection equipment. List your "must have" items and the "it would be nice to have but, we don't really need them," items.

For information about car safety features, recalls, crash tests, and other auto safety topics, go to the National Highway Traffic Safety Administration's (NHTSA) Web site at *www.nhtsa.dot.gov*. You can also call NHTSA's toll-free Auto Safety Hotline at (888) 327–4236 and have information sent to you.

COMPARISON SHOP

It has never been easier to comparison-shop and fully research your options. Read *Consumer Reports* (*www.consumerreports.org*), *Popular Mechanics* (*www.popularmechanics.com*), and *Motor Trend* (*www.motortrend.com*) for performance, service, and safety ratings. Visit *www.autoweb.com*, *www.autovantage.com*, *www.carpoint.com*, *www.autobytel.com*, or, my personal favorite, *www.Edmunds.com*, to get quotes and tons of detailed information about the entire car-buying process. The most important information that these sites provide, in my opinion, are the financial details between manufacturers and the car dealers. For instance, you can learn what a dealer gets paid by a manufacturer when a vehicle is sold within a certain period of time. This is called a dealer holdback.

Two key things to look for are the dealer's invoice price for the car and the cost of options. The invoice price is what the manufacturer charged the dealer for the car, not counting any rebates, allowances, or other incentives that reduce the cost to the dealer. The dealer will almost always receive some sort of incentives that will lower their cost below the invoice price.

So, while you will never really know the dealer's true cost, you will be close. You will be able to find out if the manufacturer is offering rebates that will lower the cost as well as any special financing offers. You should also research the MSRP, which is the base price of a particular vehicle before options and delivery charges are factored in. Your goal is to avoid paying the MSRP.

After you narrow your search to a few makes and models, analyze the pros and cons for each. Check out the retail value, fair market value, and wholesale value, available options, performance, and track record for repairs.

MAXIMIZE YOUR TRADE-IN

Before you begin to negotiate your purchase, don't forget to do the same type of research on the vehicle you plan to trade-in. This is very important. You need to get the maximum possible trade-in price. You'll have your work cut out for you. Dealer representatives will look for a thousand things wrong with your trade-in, from high mileage to minor scratches, in order to lower the value. The more prepared you are, the easier time you will have.

You will almost always make more money on your used car by selling it yourself. It is definitely less convenient than trading it in at the dealer. However, you could easily earn an extra $1,000 to $5,000 for your used car by selling it yourself. You have to decide how hard you are willing to work for that amount of money. Consider, also, that extra money used as a down payment will reduce the amount you have to borrow and pay interest on over the life of your car loan.

NEGOTIATE WITH ATTITUDE

Armed with your research, you can now begin to negotiate with people who are selling automobiles. Even the best-prepared consumer can have a difficult time once they get face to face with trained salespeople. A salesperson will size you up immediately and the price you end up paying could have a lot to do with your attitude and demeanor during the entire process. You must send a clear message right from the start that you are friendly, but well prepared; you know your stuff, and will only pay a fair price for the vehicle.

In order to save a great deal of your valuable time, and start to send the message that you plan to control the buying process, I suggest you begin by getting price quotes from several dealers via telephone, fax, or e-mail. This will also allow you to create a competitive bidding process for your business. As you will learn from your research, the "factory invoice price" is the same for all dealers of the brand of vehicle you are interested in buying. This will be your reference point and you should make it a point to tell the salesperson that you will expect to see the actual factory invoice for any car you consider buying. When you request your quote, you should also ask for a list of any additional charges that are not listed on the factory invoice. This would include dealer add-ons like document preparation, options, special handling, rust-proofing, and anything else that would increase the total price of the car. Ask if the amounts quoted are the prices before or after the rebates are deducted.

You are bound to be told by some salespeople that they aren't allowed to give out prices over the phone, or they will beat any price you can find. They will always ask you how much you are looking to pay for the car. They will, most likely, all tell you that they offer the lowest rates of any dealer in town. Just be honest with them; tell them that if they don't want to provide a price quote, you will not consider their dealership. Explain that your time for shopping is very limited and assure them you are a serious buyer.

You will eventually have to go to the dealership to complete the purchase. Never buy anything, especially very expensive items, on impulse or because the salesperson is pressuring you to make a decision. Be sure to read and understand every document you are asked to sign and never sign anything until you have made a final decision to buy.

The dealer will try to bundle your trade-in, purchase price, and financing all together once they find out how much you are willing to pay and how much you can qualify for as a monthly payment. Handle these three as separate transactions from each other to get the best deal on each one.

Be sure to read the "Buyer's Guide" sticker required to be displayed in the window of the car. It gives information on warranties, if any are offered, and provides other information, such as standard equipment included in the purchase price, delivery charges, fuel economy, and the total "sticker price." The total sticker price is MSRP plus option costs, delivery costs, and adjustments. Be on the lookout for the second sticker, often referred to as the "sucker sticker." The dealer may add all sorts of additional charges to the sticker price to boost profit. Offering to give you a discount off of the second sticker price is a common tactic but is not doing you any favors financially. If the "warranty" box is checked off on the "Buyers Guide," ask for a copy and review it before you agree to buy the car.

Test-drive several models before you make a final choice, and once you make a final choice, inspect and test-drive the vehicle you plan to buy very carefully. Once you drive it off of the lot you lose a great deal of leverage to get small dings and other repairs done for free. Be careful of salespeople who tell you to take the car home and make an appointment to have something fixed at a later date. If they want to sell you the car, they can take care of the item now. There are some exceptions. You may order an option, which has to be special ordered before being installed. You may want to take the car until the option is delivered if it is going to take a few days or weeks.

CLOSING THE DEAL

Eventually you will decide to go ahead and make a purchase and the next phase of the transaction begins. First of all, don't be misled into thinking that you have an automatic three-day cancellation period for all purchases. It is a commonly used tactic to push you into a sale by telling you that you can change your mind within three days and cancel the contract. You can only legally cancel a few types of contracts. Check your state's laws regarding contract cancellation. By the same token, you should never take possession of the car until the financing paperwork is final. You take a risk of having the deal changed on you. Maybe a higher interest rate or a few extra thousand dollars of down payment might suddenly have to be added to get the deal financed. If you already are using the car, you lose leverage.

It is a very good idea for you to shop in advance for good financing deals at your credit union, bank, or local finance company. When you finance a car, the finance charge must be stated as an Annual Percentage Rate (APR). Compare the APR and total finance charge offered by independent financial institutions with the financing offered by the dealer. You should be looking at the total cost, not just the monthly payment.

Avoid high-profit, low-value extras sold by dealers, such as credit insurance, extended service contracts, auto club memberships, rust-proofing, and upholstery finishes. You do not have to purchase credit insurance in order to get a loan. The other items are generally available for much less outside of the car dealership.

Dealers will always try to sell you an "extended warranty" or service contract when you buy a new or used car. A warranty comes with a new car and is included in the original price of the vehicle. A service contract is sold separately and is a promise to pay for certain repairs or services. Service contracts are usually high-profit add-ons, costing hundreds of dollars to more than $1,000. The service contract may duplicate warranty coverage you get from the manufacturer or dealer. For that matter, an extended warranty may duplicate coverage by the manufacturer's warranty.

If you choose to purchase extended service, you will want to know who is responsible for providing the outlined services: the dealer, the manufacturer, or an independent company. Don't assume that it is automatically the dealer. Ask and understand what happens to your coverage if the dealer or administrator goes out of business. Learn the process for how repair claims will be handled and make sure you fully understand if you will be responsible for paying any additional deductible or co-payments or service fees.

The service contract may prohibit you from taking your car to an independent station for routine maintenance or performing the work yourself. That might include very basic service like changing the oil, which is usually more expensive if it has to be done at the dealer's service center. You may also be required to have your vehicle serviced on a scheduled basis whether you think you need it or not. Failure to keep up manufacturer's recommendations for routine maintenance can void the service contract and you'll be out the money you paid for it.

Make sure your service contract can travel with you to another state if you travel or move out of town. Watch out for exclusions that deny coverage for any reason and other terms that could cost extra when repairs are made.

CONSIDERING A USED CAR?

As we've discussed, used cars offer you the best chance to own the car of your dreams at an affordable price. The biggest issue with buying a used vehicle is its condition. If you have automotive repair skills, or are close to someone who does, buying a used car is a little safer. For the majority of us, buying a used car is much more of a risk. There are companies and individuals who will check out used cars before you purchase them for a fee. It is probably not a good idea to ask the dealer for recommendations. You will have to find these experts on your own. Often your bank could be helpful. A local mechanic at a service station you are familiar with could be helpful but you really need to check and verify his credentials and experience.

Once you find a mechanic you trust and are comfortable working with, you can begin to search for an acceptable used car. It is a good idea to check the classifieds, *Auto Trader Magazine,* and the Internet for used cars. Finding a used vehicle that is in good, clean condition will take time and energy. Any required repairs will help you bring your offer price down since you will have the expense of bringing the car back to proper condition. Look at the vehicle very closely and note any and all damage or problems. This is where your mechanic can earn his weight in gold.

There are some other, smart-buyer strategies you should use when buying used cars. Seek a dealer that covers used cars with at least a thirty-day, 100 percent warranty where the dealer agrees to pay all repair costs for covered items. Try to avoid "As Is—No Warranty" cars. Some states have laws giving extra protection to used-car buyers. Contact your state or local consumer protection office to find out what rights you have.

Check with your state's department of motor vehicles for information on the car's title history. Make sure the car is not a "lemon buy-back," salvaged, or wrecked car. You should insist on getting a written mileage disclosure statement. This is required by federal law from any seller and you should be sure it matches the odometer reading on the car. It is always a good idea to check the title to the car before you sign on the dotted line.

If you are buying from a private individual you should understand that private sellers generally have less responsibility than dealers for defects or other problems. Make sure the seller isn't a dealer posing as an individual. That might mean the dealer is trying to evade the law and might be an indicator of problems with the car. Look closely at the title and registration. Make sure the seller is the registered owner of the vehicle. It is really important to ask the seller lots of detailed questions about the car.

SHOULD YOU LEASE?

In recent years, leasing has become a very popular way for people to afford to drive automobiles. Once reserved exclusively for business people and companies that needed fleets of automobiles, leasing was introduced to the general public and quickly has become a popular way for consumers to afford newer and more luxurious vehicles. In fact, leasing is the choice in about 28 percent of all new-car transactions.

I am, personally, a fan of leasing for many reasons. I remember distinctly when I became interested in leasing. It was the day I mailed in the last payment on the last car I had purchased and financed. That day, I was at an automotive service center getting a $600 estimate for fixing the air conditioning on the car. The air-conditioning system had stopped working the day before. That was the day I realized what a bad investment cars can be; after a while, they break down and start costing a lot of money to keep running. Even if it doesn't break down, it is an old car.

Leasing is not the perfect choice for everyone. It really has to be a decision based on your lifestyle and spending plan. For example, now that my oldest son, Drew, is about four years away from wanting a car of his own, I am seriously considering purchasing my next car so that I would be able to pass it onto him when he is ready.

These are the basic differences between leasing and buying. When you lease, you pay to drive someone else's vehicle. Leasing is just a fancy word for renting. Although leasing usually provides for lower monthly payments than a loan, at lease end, you have no ownership or equity in the car. With a lease, you don't pay interest or finance charges as you do on a loan, but you do pay rent charges, which are calculated using the lease rate or "money factor." The money factor is used to calculate the leasing company's monthly fee (the rent charge). Clearly, your goal is to negotiate the lowest possible money factor or lease rate.

The Consumer Leasing Act requires leasing companies to disclose standardized information to lease customers. In addition to the information disclosed on a standardized form, you should always ask for an itemization of the capitalized cost. You should shop as if you're buying a car. You want to know your total payments with interest over the term of the lease. Understand that you may negotiate all the lease terms, including the price of the vehicle, how many miles per year are included in the lease, the down payment, and the purchase option price at the end of the lease. Lowering the lease price will help reduce your monthly payments.

You will receive the terms of the lease in writing. Be sure to pay close attention to the leasing company's standards for wear and use. Tire wear and dings that you may regard as normal wear and tear may be billed as significant damage at the end of your lease.

You can expect to pay a substantial charge if you give the car up before the end of your lease. Most leases allow you to drive 12,000 to 15,000 miles a year and then you are responsible for a charge of ten to twenty-five cents for each additional mile. You do not pay for the mileage at the end of each year so don't get too hung up on it unless you drive a lot of miles every year. If you use your vehicle for typical driving, you should look at the total mileage you are given in the lease. For example, if you are given 12,000 free miles each year, and the lease is for three years, you have a total of 36,000 miles you can drive. The last year of the lease is when you might have to make some adjustments in your driving so you don't go over the allotted amount.

One of the things I like about new-car leases is that the manufacturer's warranty covers the entire lease term. If something breaks, you are covered while you are leasing the car. When you purchase a car, your warranty coverage could end while you are still making payments on the vehicle, leaving you totally responsible for the cost of repairs.

Be sure to get every item of equipment included with the car listed on the lease. Otherwise, you could be charged for "missing" equipment at the end of the lease. Be careful to review your lease for any charges that were not disclosed by the salesperson, like conveyance, disposition, and preparation fees. Make sure you get credit for any trade-in just as you would with a purchase.

When you finance a car, the finance charge must be stated as an APR. There is no similar requirement for disclosing the cost of leases. "Lease rates" or "money factors" do not have standardized definitions and are not equivalent to an APR.

Your lease agreement will disclose the rent charge. Be sure this amount is explained to you and that you understand all charges fully before you sign the lease agreement.

Another great reason to lease is the tax savings. Sales tax, in most states, is only paid on the lease payments rather than the full price of the vehicle. The shorter the lease term, the more sales tax you save compared with purchasing the vehicle. If you buy a vehicle and wrap the sales tax into the financing, you will pay interest on top of the sales tax.

To buy or to lease is a question to answer by using your spending plan and deciding where you want to be financially at the end of the lease or purchase financing term. It may make more sense, based on your spending plan, for you to lease. Lower monthly payments and no cash out of pocket may be more important right now than having a used vehicle worth a few thousand dollars in three to five years. If you lease, at the end of the lease you will have to deal with these same decisions again. If you buy a vehicle, there is a good chance that you will get a few years after you pay off the loan where you may not have a car payment. If you find yourself in that position, I urge you to continue to pay yourself that monthly payment that you have become used to making and living without. Use it to pay down debt or as a down payment to buy a new home. Keep in mind that, eventually, your vehicle will wear out and you will need to get another one. Perhaps the idea of having a new vehicle every two to three years is appealing enough to you to not mind having a perpetual car payment. As long as you plan the payments into your monthly and yearly spending plans you can drive the car you want to drive on the financial terms that work best for you and your family.

8

$ $

Join the Smart Shopper's Club

"Anytime you can band together with other consumers in the marketplace, you have the advantage of being able to shape the buying experience, the pricing, and the types of products offered."

Discount-buying clubs are more popular than ever and provide consumers like you and me the opportunity to save money on just about everything we need to buy. There are many types of discount-buying clubs in existence today. Most of them were created specifically to serve shoppers but many discount-buying clubs began simply as a way for merchants to cut their advertising costs and still reach a large number of people. In either case, they give us more chances to be Power Buyers.

ORGANIZATIONAL DISCOUNTS

If you are part of an organization of any size, whether for business or pleasure, you most likely have had the opportunity to receive discounts simply because you are a member of the group. Retailers realize it makes sense to offer discounts to large affinity groups since they can reach a large number of people with their message. Members of the group tend to be more receptive to the offers. Many times, the merchant is a member of the group. Think about it—aren't you more receptive to advertising messages that come in your group's monthly newsletter? Don't you appreciate merchants that make offers of special savings to your group?

As with most things, there is power in numbers and this is especially true when it comes to dealing with manufacturers and retailers. Anytime you can band together with other consumers in the marketplace, you have the advantage of being able to shape the buying experience, the pricing, and the types of products offered. It always makes sense to take advantage of group savings opportunities. If you are a member of a large organization that is not getting special offers for its members, your leaders are not doing a good job of taking care of the membership. Special group discounts are something you should expect and demand. Leverage the power of your group with as many merchants and manufacturers as possible in order to get better prices on things you want and need. In my opinion, often the best reason to join some groups is specifically for the discounts that the organization has negotiated for its membership. One of the best ways to attract members to your organization is by offering great benefits to members. You can create a win-win-win situation. Your organization can grow its membership, the members benefit from being part of a great organization and having access to good benefits, and the merchants benefit by getting exposure to a large number of people at relatively low cost.

THE BURGEONING WAREHOUSE CLUB

The fastest growing segment of the discount-buying club concept, where members get special discounts and money-saving offers, is the huge discount warehouse clubs like Sam's Club, Costco Wholesale, and BJ's Wholesale Club. Forget the old jokes about having to buy a dozen pairs of socks to save a few dollars. The warehouse stores have listened to consumers and now offer everyone the opportunity to save a great deal of money on everything from jewelry to gasoline. You can benefit from club membership even if you are single and don't have a big family for which you are buying.

It is estimated that warehouse club members save at least 25 percent a year over buying from traditional retail outlets. This makes the average $35 annual membership fee a big bargain. Our family saves much more than 25 percent on most of the items that we buy regularly, so I believe the actual average savings is higher for the typical family.

The shopping experience at these warehouse stores is different from the typical retail store. They are big and very open inside without being very pretty. The presentation plays second fiddle to lower pricing. The original business model of these stores was to cut out all of the expensive overhead costs and buy and sell items in bulk in order to reduce prices. No coupons, other than those created by the warehouse clubs themselves are accepted; credit cards were not accepted in the beginning to in order to avoid the fees involved with processing those sales. Anything that would require extra expense on the part of the warehouse company was eliminated, if possible, in order to keep product prices low. You still will not find perfumed store clerks standing around waiting to answer questions. Stock people are usually busy stocking products but will usually take time to point you in the right direction if you are lost inside the store. And the biggest surprise of all, you have to box or bag your own purchases, and carry them out to the car yourself.

This really was not a new idea. Bulk-buying direct from the manufacturer has been done for centuries. Business owners were used to buying in bulk direct from manufacturers in a no-frills setting, usually right off of the manufacturing floor. Small business owners were among the first to flock to the warehouse stores to buy bulk products for resale at their own stores. That is how good the prices are. That was also the original way to be invited to be a member of the club. Membership was offered through companies to their employees. That has changed and membership is now open to the public.

The warehouse concept was unusual, however, to the typical retail shopper who had gotten used to the pretty surroundings and ambiance of the suburban mall stores. But, if you can overcome your need for mood lighting and expensive decorations, you will save huge amounts of money at the warehouse clubs without giving up quality. In fact, of all the opportunities to upgrade your lifestyle by spending less, I would rate the warehouse clubs at the top of the list. You can buy better-quality products and services and truly upgrade your lifestyle by becoming a member.

WAREHOUSE CLUB SPENDING STRATEGIES

Of course, anytime you put yourself in position to spend money, you still need to be a smart shopper. Even if you are in a store that is designed to provide discounts, you must make sure you are not getting caught up in the hype and are truly getting good prices. There is also more of a danger to impulse buy at these big discount stores. You are surrounded by low prices on quality items. It would be easy to start to justify overspending because of the great deals. Following these simple strategies will help keep you in line with your spending plan:

➤ While it is fun to shop randomly in the warehouse stores looking for great deals, just as you do with ordinary, retail shopping trips, you should preplan your shopping, especially if you are looking for specific items that are more costly, like computers, televisions, or appliances. Do some pre-shopping research so you know what product features, benefits, and capabilities you want and need, and how much the product normally costs at retail establishments and on the Internet.

➤ Be prepared to compare food products ounce for ounce with grocery store prices. Just because something is offered in a larger container doesn't automatically make it a great deal for the price.

Keep your family's actual consumption habits in mind at all times. If the store accepts coupons, use them. If bulk items are a good deal, make sure they have an extended shelf life or can be frozen until you need them. Getting a great price on something that won't last until you need it is wasting money. As with grocery stores, the store brand is usually cheaper without much difference in quality. However, don't assume that paying the lowest price is always the best way to go. I believe in enjoying the things you buy so it makes no sense to me to pay less but not like what you bought.

➤ While you will have a variety of products to choose from, you will find less choice in each product group. The warehouse stores pride themselves on negotiating the best deals on certain brands of products, cutting out the middleman, and buying those products in bulk to get the best prices. The goal is to sell out those lots as quickly as possible. Sometimes the deals are so good at these stores you will experience a frenzied atmosphere in certain areas of the store. I see this quite a bit in the clothing section where brand-name clothes usually sell at incredible discounts compared to retail prices. When an especially good price is offered, the merchandise really moves quickly, even without changing rooms available for buyers to try on the items. The return policies in these stores—and we shop in all three of them regularly—are excellent. They just don't waste time arguing with customers if the product does not meet the customer's needs. I've even noticed that employees at these stores have a better attitude than employees at traditional retail stores.

➤ Shopping at your local warehouse club once a month is a good idea. Plus, not everything you need will be available at a great price at the club so you will still have to use other stores to meet all of your needs.

One of the most common questions I've been asked is whether I thought it is necessary to join all of the warehouse clubs in town, or, if joining just one is enough. I find that the different clubs appeal to different people for a variety of reasons. It might be the product selection, layout of the stores, or, the location. We find that we like the produce from one club, the meats from another, and other types of products from the third. So, we belong to three of them and visit the one that offers the products for which we are shopping. I think you can do just fine with a membership in one of the warehouse clubs. If you are lucky enough to have a choice, it is not necessary to join every one of them in your city. I suggest you take a trial visit to each club and decide in which one you feel most comfortable.

DISCOUNT CLUBS ON THE INTERNET

Discount-buying clubs also have arrived on the Internet. While there are many places to find free coupons, rebates, and discounts for just about every type of product and service available on the Internet, there are also many online companies that provide access to savings and discounts through buyer's clubs or other types of membership programs. Internet-based discount-buying clubs, which you pay some enrollment fee to join, give you access to money-saving offers in specific categories like travel, groceries, and medical care. Some of the more sophisticated savings programs will provide you with a membership card that can be used to receive discounts when you shop at different merchants in your area. You will be able to search the company's Internet site using your zip code to find savings offers on different products and services within each category.

If you have ever purchased one of those discount savings books from a student trying to raise money for school, you know the concept of a discount-buying program. It is much more powerful on the Internet because these programs actually allow you to be very specific in your search for discounts on particular items. You are given access to order coupons a specified number of times a month for your membership fee. The better programs provide you with unlimited use of the site. If you are using the service regularly for many of the things you buy, you can save hundreds of dollars a year with just a few strokes on your computer keyboard.

INCREASING YOUR FAMILY'S BUYING POWER

Whatever it takes to improve your family's lifestyle, do it. Make no apologies for being a Power Buyer. If becoming a member of any club will give you the opportunity to increase your family's buying power, it is something you should consider as part of your overall spending plan. I suggest you make a visit to your local warehouse club this week and seriously consider becoming a member. While others make jokes about buying three dozen shirts and six pounds of hamburger, you will be taking yet another step toward spending your way to wealth.

If you are already a member, I congratulate you for taking advantage of the opportunity and challenge you to use even more of your membership benefits to save more money than you ever have in the coming year.

$ $ $ $ $ $ $ $ $ $ $ $ $ $ **9** $ $ $ $ $ $ $ $ $ $ $ $ $ $ $

Buy a House and Save $100,000

"People would be better off driving smaller cars and living in bigger houses."

Owning a home has been romanticized and called the "dream" of every American. Perhaps at one time in this country it was considered a dream to own a home. Now, it can be a reality for just about anyone, even on a modest income. As I write this, we are enjoying the lowest mortgage interest rates in a generation and home ownership is growing at a fast pace. This is good news because the right to own property is one of the principals our country was founded upon.

I also believe it is very important for each family to own their home, because owning a home provides a great deal of foundation for the family. Families, in my opinion, need to have a sense of belonging, especially when children are involved. A home of their own provides a special feeling that is missing when a family rents a place to live. A rented home or apartment never feels totally like home. You can get used to it after a while, but why settle for less when you can truly have a home of your own?

Buying your own home is one of the purest ways to spend your way to wealth. However, there is a great deal of difference between being the legally recognized owner of a home and having a true, equitable position in a property. There are so many special loan programs in existence that just about anyone can qualify for a mortgage to buy a house, on just about any income. But, if you pay too much for a house, or buy a home in a declining neighborhood, you may never enjoy the financial benefits you could have if you make smart decisions from the start.

This chapter will help make you a smarter real estate investor. I'll bet some of you never thought of it in that way. "A real estate investor? But, I'm a homeowner," you may be thinking. "Investors buy property as a business, don't they?"

If you own property, you are investing in real estate. Even if you own only your primary residence, you are a real-estate investor. I find it very interesting how few people realize this concept. When we talk about investing in general and the question comes up, "How much of your investment portfolio includes real estate?" a common answer is, "Well, we don't have any real estate investments." Then, I ask if the person owns her home and the lights start to go on. Your biggest investment is probably your home. The median price for a home in the United States as of this writing is about $155,000 and more than $300,000 in the state of California. To buy that property, you will need at least 5 percent and perhaps 10 to 20 percent of that amount in cash to invest into the deal. When you take into account the down payment, closing costs, and fix-up costs, you might have spent $20,000 to $45,000 in cash for your initial investment in your home. That is a great deal of money to have invested in real estate. Many do not have that much money saved in a 401k or other retirement fund, or any other investment, for that matter. And, with a home, you literally are investing more money into it every week just to maintain it.

Even if you bought a home that was much less expensive than the median price level, you were still required to make quite an investment. Add up all the cash you have put into the purchase and compare that investment against other investments you may have. I think you will find that you have a substantial stake in real estate as part of your total investment portfolio. And, if you do not have any investment in real estate, you are missing an opportunity for incredible returns on investment.

According to the National Association of Realtors, $20,000 invested in the S&P 500 in April 1992 would have been worth $52,694 in ten years while the same investment in a home would have yielded $75,133.

HOME EQUITY: THE BEST REASON TO OWN

There are many reasons people give for not owning a home. They feel that they don't have enough money for a down payment. Houses are too expensive or they don't feel they have good enough credit. Buying and owning a home takes more work than renting. Fear of the legal aspect of negotiating and completing a real estate transaction is also a reason many prefer to rent. I've heard people tell me they were too young to own a home, while others felt that they were too old. The bottom line is, you can think of hundreds of reasons not to do something. But, if you have one compelling reason to do it, then you can motivate yourself through any obstacles.

Here is the most compelling reason to own real estate: Owning a home can give you great financial power and leverage as your equity grows. Home equity loans and home equity lines of credit become available to people with equity in their homes. Equity is important. Equity is simply the difference between what the house can sell for and what you owe on the property. Home equity is a powerful financial tool that is instrumental in helping people to pay off their debt at lower interest rates, start businesses, pay for college education, retire comfortably, and much more. Many people will generate more future wealth through real estate than they will by saving money in a 401k retirement plan. Think about this for a moment. You can literally start the day off reading your newspaper's classified ads and within a week or two end up with thousands of dollars in home equity at your disposal. It can happen with real estate. You can buy and sell a home and earn several thousand dollars in a very short time frame. In less than a month, you can turn home equity into cash. That is powerful. But, as with all spending and investing, you must do it correctly from the beginning. Any real estate expert would tell you that you make money in real estate when you buy a piece of property and you realize the money when you sell the property. This is a key concept. You make money when you buy so you must do it correctly. The world is full of people who own property that is worth less now than when they bought it. You want to avoid this situation by being a smart real-estate investor. We'll do our best to get you started on the right foot.

It is very important to buy a home with built-in equity right from the start. That is, it is worth more than what you are buying it for to begin with. It is very important to understand that it does not matter what you personally think the house is worth. What matters most is what the market says the house is worth. If all of the homes that have sold in a neighborhood in the past twelve months have sold for $80,000, the market is setting a level for home prices in that neighborhood at around $80,000. If you buy a home for $90,000, you have overbought and chances are very good that you will not be able to get your money out of the home if you sell it any time in the near future because you would have to sell it for more than $90,000. Your goal would be to buy a home in this neighborhood for under $80,000.

Equity is crucial to your decision on buying a property. Savvy real estate investors make it a rule never to buy property at the top price of any market or neighborhood and, certainly, never if the home is priced above the market level. It happens, though. People buy homes every day that are overpriced. There is always a better deal to be had if you don't get emotionally involved in making such an important investment decision.

The numbers must add up in your favor in a real estate transaction. If you buy a home that is in a declining neighborhood, too run down, and requiring costly repairs, or simply one that is overpriced compared to similar homes in the area, it will be nearly impossible for your investment to grow in value.

STOP SUBSIDIZING YOUR LANDLADY

I am not going to spend an excessive amount of time in this chapter discussing the various nuts and bolts of real estate transactions and mortgage negotiations. There are many good books on those subjects from noted experts like Robert Allen, Russ Witney, Robert Kiyosaki, and Carleton Sheets. I do want to spend time alerting you to what I believe are the key factors in properly buying a home, negotiating for the best possible mortgage, and using the home's equity to your financial advantage. The bottom line is if you do not own the place you are living in, it is costing you a lot of money now, and will continue to do so in the future. This chapter is important if you want to increase your financial power and at the same time put thousands of dollars into your bank account.

Let's talk about the basic decision of renting versus owning. This is a simple concept and really not a decision at all. You are buying a home whether you rent or buy. If you are renting, you are just not buying the home for the benefit of you or your family. You are buying the home for the landlady and her family. You are helping the landlady build her equity so that she may use that equity to her financial advantage. You get no advantage when you rent, other than a roof over your head.

In most cases, you are not only paying off the landlady's mortgage, you are actually overpaying by a certain percentage, which is mostly profit for the landlady. Renting property is a business with expenses, so you've got to have some profit in the deal if you rent properties and hope to continue to do so. The renters must pay more than is required to simply cover the mortgage, in order to cover expenses and provide a profit to the landlady.

In apartment buildings, the profit margin is huge. Just imagine the profit on a single apartment in a big apartment complex that cost maybe $5,000 to $10,000 to build and is then rented for the next twenty to fifty years or more! There are apartment buildings across the country that are hundreds of years old. The mortgages on those properties have long since been satisfied and now the rents are generating pure profit for the owner. Just think of the incredible wealth creation going on with year after year of rental payments coming in, with profit built in, plus the equity growth of the property as the mortgage is paid down by the renters. The margins aren't so big on single-family homes, but they can also be very profitable as rentals. And don't forget, the landlady also gets tax deductions, which can be taken on the estimated depreciation of the rental property. More financial advantage for her, less for you.

Certainly, there are times when renting may be appropriate for a short period of time. Perhaps you have just moved to a new city and want to take some time to decide where to invest in a home. Or you need to sell your home quickly for some reason and need to move out before you can make a good decision on buying a new home. These are legitimate short-term uses of rental property. I am merely saying that you shouldn't get used to it. There are many more reasons to buy your own home than to rent a place. If you have to do it for a legitimate reason, just don't get used to it and do it for too long.

Building future wealth through increasing equity is one of the biggest reasons to own your own home, as we have discussed. But let's not forget about the opportunities to keep more money in your pocket right now through home ownership.

Reducing your tax burden through home ownership gives you an opportunity to increase your take-home pay right away. When you create allowable tax deductions, reducing the amount of income tax you will owe, you can adjust your W-4 form at work, which will reduce the amount of money taken out of your paycheck each week to pay income taxes.

BUYING FSBOS

Let's discuss some winning home buying strategies that will help you from the beginning to buy property properly to maximize your wealth-building potential. To save yourself 3 to 7 percent right off of the top of the selling price of a home, buy properties that are for sale by owner. These are known as FSBOs in the industry. People who choose to sell their homes themselves are actively attempting to save money by not using a real-estate listing agent who charges a commission. There are several reasons to explain why they may be doing this. They could be very astute followers of my radio show and realize how smart it is to avoid paying those thousands of dollars in real-estate agent commissions. More often than not, though, these FSBO sellers are doing it themselves because they can't afford to use an agent.

You see, if a seller uses a real-estate listing agent, the seller automatically has to add the sales commission to the selling price of the home because the commission comes from the proceeds of the sale. When someone uses a listing agent, the mortgage payoff balance has to be at least 10 percent under the selling price just to break even. Otherwise, the seller will have to start digging into his own pockets to cover the costs for selling the house because a listing agent will get up to 7 percent of the selling price right off of the top. Then, the portion of the seller's closing costs are usually in the range of 3 to 5 percent of the home's selling price. If a seller needs most of the selling price proceeds for his own purposes, such as to pay off the current mortgage, debts, or other expense, it will be difficult for him to pay a sales commission out of the sales price.

When a seller puts the home up for sale by himself, there is often more flexibility in the selling price, and you always save the commissions. Even though the seller technically pays the commission out of the sales proceeds, you, the buyer, are really paying the bill since you are buying the home.

QUESTIONS TO ASK A SELLER

Here are some key questions to ask a seller that will give you an advantage when deciding how much to offer for a home. You need to find out how much the seller needs from the sale of the home, why he needs the money, and what his mortgage payoff balance is currently. You can find out some of this information by searching your county tax records either online or where they keep the physical tax and real-estate ownership records in your city or county.

In the tax records you can also research the selling prices of similar homes in the neighborhood, as well as how much the seller originally paid for a property. This is very valuable information that you must have in order to be a smart real estate investor. You should also check out any other houses for sale in the neighborhood that are using listing agents. They will provide you with lots of valuable information about the sales environment in the area in which you are interested in living.

ADVANTAGES OF PRE-APPROVAL

While you are searching for a home, it is a good idea to start shopping for a good mortgage offer and get pre-qualified and approved for a mortgage so you can act quickly once you find a property you are interested in buying. Being pre-approved for a mortgage is much stronger than being pre-qualified. Anyone can pre-qualify you by looking at a couple of key pieces of financial information such as your credit score, your monthly gross income, and unsecured debt balances and expenses. You can easily pre-qualify yourself. All pre-qualification means is that you have met some preliminary qualifying parameters. Being pre-approved means the lender has gone more deeply into your qualifications and has provided assurance to you that you may have a loan at a specific interest rate when you are ready to make a purchase.

It is prudent to shop several banks, starting with the one with which you have your checking account. Also, interview several mortgage brokers, looking for one with which you feel comfortable working. While banks can provide you with a mortgage loan, they will be more limited in the number and types of loan programs they have to offer. A good mortgage broker, on the other hand, will have thousands of programs from which to choose. Mortgage brokers are very competitive and need to hustle for business, while local banks are less aggressive. If you are like me, you will want someone who is going to work hard for you and treat you like you are their only customer. I demand this type of treatment and let them know right from the start what I expect. A real estate transaction has too big of a financial impact on my family to fool around with inexperienced or uninterested people. They work for me while the transaction is being completed, so I expect a focused and serious effort on my behalf.

Mortgage lenders and brokers perform a very needed service, and good ones can put together loans that can be very good for your finances. But, in the end, they are commissioned salespeople, so review any recommendations carefully to make sure the person getting the best deal in the deal is you. Check all proposed fees and costs very carefully. Virtually every cost included in a mortgage good-faith estimate, which is a preliminary estimate of all of the costs you will pay for the mortgage closing, including the interest rate, are negotiable. Be prepared to wince at each cost on the estimate and don't be afraid to ask if the broker or lender can do better. Watch out for double charges on such things as application fees and administrative fees. Ask what each cost will cover and why it is needed.

By the way, the higher your credit score, the more power you will have to negotiate with mortgage lenders and brokers. I suggest you don't wait to apply for your mortgage to take a look at your credit report and credit score. The time to do something about a less-than-perfect credit history is before you apply for loans. Once you initiate the process, it is impossible to make any improvements in your credit score quickly enough to affect the outcome on the current loan.

AVOIDING PMI

A good mortgage professional will also understand how to help you structure your loan to eliminate the need for private mortgage insurance (PMI). Avoiding the requirement to pay for PMI is very important. Private mortgage insurance is one of the hidden costs of a mortgage loan. It costs you money that would be better spent on extra principle payments, paying off credit card debt, saving, or just about any other positive use you can think of. This insurance policy is required by most lenders if you make a down payment of less than 20 percent or if your loan balance on the home you already own is less than 20 percent of the home's market value. It provides protection only for the lender in case of a default on the mortgage loan and does not help the homeowner at all. Still, the homeowner is required to pay the premium year after year. That money is simply gone. It is an expense that can reduce your disposable income by several hundred to several thousand dollars a year and give you nothing in return. In my opinion, it punishes good people more than it penalizes the people who default on their mortgages and create the need for this insurance in the first place. In fact, the more responsible you are in making your mortgage payments, the more of a rip-off this insurance is. You may have owned a home for thirty years and never missed a payment, but, if you buy a new home and put less than 20 percent down, you will be required to have private mortgage insurance. If your mortgage is FHA- or VA-guaranteed, you are also required to pay a mortgage insurance premium (MIP). To add insult to injury, mortgage insurance is not deductible from your taxes like mortgage interest is.

While this insurance has been credited for making it possible for many more people to own homes because it reduces the lender's risk, it comes at a high price for homeowners. First, there is an up-front premium required of 1.5 percent of the purchase price for FHA-, VA-, and FmHA-backed mortgage loans. That equals $1,500 on a $100,000 home. The lender will be happy to wrap that amount into the thirty-year mortgage so you will be paying interest on top of the premium amount. The initial premium for a conventional loan is usually around half of a percent of the total sales price. Then, the renewal cost of the policy each year ranges from one third of a percent to one half of a percent of the loan balance. That is an extra $300 to $500 a year on a $100,000 balance.

By the way, you do not get to shop for the best premium; the lender will choose the insurer. And, you can't even see the policy because it is not your policy. You just pay the bill.

Even when a homeowner does reach 20 percent equity, the lender does not automatically cancel the PMI. The homeowner must request that the policy be canceled. According to congressional testimony, overpayment of PMI is potentially costing hundreds of thousands of homeowners millions of dollars per year.

I am happy to report that there are ways to eliminate the requirement for PMI. The easiest way to avoid the requirement is to put a 20 percent down payment on your home loan. Most people, however, cannot afford that much of a down payment and the lenders know it. According to Freddie Mac, the average down payment by first-time homebuyers is just 10 percent.

One great way to avoid the PMI requirement involves getting a first mortgage for 80 percent of your loan, with a 10 percent down payment, and a second mortgage to cover the other 10 percent of the down payment, giving you a total down payment of 20 percent. This is sometimes called a "piggy-back" mortgage. Since your first mortgage is at 80 percent loan-to-value, the requirement for mortgage insurance is eliminated. A good mortgage broker, who is up on the latest programs and strategies, can help you accomplish this.

Some lenders offer a loan that actually builds the PMI into the interest rate. You would have to agree to pay a higher interest rate but the interest cost is tax deductible.

Without the PMI requirement, you can save thousands of dollars in interest because you can put the money you would be paying toward insurance for the lender right into the principle of your loan. Or, you could spend the money on presents for your children. Anything is better than having to pay a monthly fee to insure your lender.

Thanks to the Homeowners' Protection Act of 1998, PMI on all mortgages issued after July 1999 automatically cancels when you reach 22 percent equity in your home. Don't wait for the extra 2 percent growth in your equity, though. Waiting could end up costing you hundreds or thousands of dollars in additional insurance payments. The Homeowners' Protection Act requires lenders to notify you when your home equity reaches 20 percent. The minute you get the notification request the cancellation of the PMI. If your mortgage was issued prior to 1999, it is your responsibility to keep track of when your equity reaches 20 percent in order to take action to have the PMI requirement cancelled.

By the way, if you have ever had a HUD/FHA-insured mortgage, you may be eligible for a refund on part of your insurance premium payments or a share of the earnings of the mutual mortgage insurance fund in which your payments were invested. To find out if the government owes you some money, just call the U.S. Department of Housing and Urban Development at (800) 697–6967, or visit online *www.hud.gov.*

CUT THE COST OF HOMEOWNER'S INSURANCE

One other area where you can save substantially is also insurance related. You will be required by your lender to also carry Homeowner's Insurance to protect your home from catastrophic loss or damage. This insurance also protects you if someone should be injured on your property. As with any insurance policy, it pays to shop around for coverage to get the lowest rates. You are dealing with salespeople again, so double-check everything. This is another big expense that the percentages show will rarely be utilized. You have to have this protection so get the best quality for the lowest price. Going with the first name in the yellow pages or the referral from the real estate agent is not the best strategy. Be sure you deal with a highly rated and well-respected company that has few complaints from homeowners. You can check with your state's insurance commissioner's office for information on good companies for all of your insurance needs.

When it comes to insurance, the higher your deductible is set, the lower your premium will be. But many are afraid to set the deductible too high for fear that they won't have the money to cover the deductible should they ever need it. Here is a strategy to help you feel more comfortable choosing a higher deductible, saving you money on your insurance premiums, while allowing you to have the money to cover the deductible in an emergency. Open a credit card account for the amount of your deductible. Suppose your deductible is $1,000. This special credit card should have a $1,000 credit limit.

Choose a card with no annual fee so it costs you nothing to carry the account. A low interest rate is also preferable. You are not going to be using this card except in an emergency, so the interest really is not that big of a concern, but, you always want to have the lowest interest rates possible. Keep this credit card locked away in a safe in your home, or in some other secure place. If you ever, unfortunately, endure a situation where your home is damaged or lost, you will always have that credit card account available to help you cover the deductible for your homeowner's insurance if you needed to use it. Then, you won't have to worry about having the cash available for the deductible in an emergency.

BUILDING REAL WEALTH!

Once you close the mortgage and become a homeowner, you are in position to begin to save thousands of dollars every year both in mortgage interest that I will show you how to eliminate, and on income taxes you will reduce due to allowable tax deductions for homeowners. Over time, by working to grow your equity in the home, you will build a valuable estate. This is how real wealth is created.

Hopefully, you have made a smart purchase by doing some homework, questioning costs, fees, and other expenses, and are already sitting on a healthy amount of equity. You have worked with a good mortgage professional and have found a loan program at the lowest-possible interest rate that is structured to eliminate the need to pay for private mortgage insurance, saving you hundreds or thousands of dollars each year. And, you have minimized your homeowner's insurance costs. This is money in your pocket that you can use to create a richer lifestyle. Wealthy people use these techniques to build fortunes.

Granted, it takes extra work on your part to get the best possible price for a home and a good mortgage. You can take the easy way out, of course. I, personally, have always felt that the toll on the easy road is much too expensive.

Now, let's talk about the really big money that you can spend without regard, or keep where it really belongs: in your account. The cost of a home, when you calculate interest, is stunning. Many people don't realize the real, total cost of a home over the long run thanks to interest. The same happens with an automobile purchase, or any expensive purchase where interest is involved. We get so fixated on the monthly payment and being sure we can afford it, that we don't realize how much things really cost over time, including interest. Since a home is, most likely, your biggest expense ever, the cost of interest on top of the principle is always a big number. But don't despair—by using some simple techniques, it is possible to save thousands of dollars in interest while you also build up equity in your home more quickly.

When you close on your loan, ask the mortgage company for what is called an amortization schedule. This is a breakdown of your payments during the life of the loan. They may charge you a small fee for this service but it is well worth it. You could also buy software to create your own or visit any number of financial Web sites that give you the ability to produce this document by entering into a worksheet information such as your loan balance, interest rate, and term of your loan.

The amortization schedule will show you all three hundred and sixty payments for a thirty-year loan. Each month's principle amount and interest amount will be broken out separately. When you add the two together, you get your monthly principle and interest payment. It is fascinating just to see what you will still owe on your home, say, ten or fifteen years from now, if you just make your regular monthly payments. You will notice that, for a long time, the interest portion of the payment is very large in comparison to a very small principle amount. As you make each payment, the next month's interest amount is a little bit smaller and the principle amount gets a little bit bigger. Eventually, the two amounts are nearly equal, then the principle becomes a bigger portion of your monthly payment while the interest portion keeps getting smaller.

The real power in this document is in realizing that by prepaying a principal amount, you eliminate the interest charge on that amount. For example, let's say your amortization schedule shows next month's principle amount at $60 and the interest amount at $700. When you make this month's regular payment, all you have to do is add next month's principle amount of $60 to your payment, and you will have effectively eliminated next month's $700 interest cost because you aren't borrowing the $60. Go to next month's payment and cross it off. You just saved yourself and your family $700. How long does it take to write out a check to your mortgage company? Seconds, right? In a matter of seconds, with a few strokes of a pen each month, you can earn hundreds of dollars in savings. The pen really is mightier than the sword! Do this each month and you will eliminate years from your mortgage and thousands of dollars in interest payments.

Here are some other ways to prepay principle, eliminate mortgage interest to save thousands and thousands of dollars, and build your home equity faster, even if you don't use an amortization schedule. Make one extra mortgage payment each year or just add some extra amount to each month's payment, which you put toward the principle. The faster you pay down the principle amount, the less you will end up paying in interest. Still not convinced that this is the right thing to do? Look at these actual numbers. I just ran these numbers in an online loan calculator while broadcasting my radio show. A $100,000 mortgage balance is calculated at 6.3 percent interest, today's average mortgage interest rate for thirty-year fixed rate loan. The monthly principal and interest payment calculates at $680.97. The total interest paid over the life of the loan, thirty years, will be $123,000. By adding just $100 more to each monthly payment, the monthly principal and interest payment would increase to $780.97, but the thirty-year loan is reduced to twenty years and eleven months. The total interest paid is reduced by more than $42,000. That is $42,000 in the homeowner's pocket or, $1,400 a year. Would an extra $100 or so a month in your account be of any use to you? You could easily pay the extra $42,000 to the mortgage company or it can stay where it belongs—in your family. This knowledge gives you great financial power. Hopefully it gets you very excited to start implementing this strategy.

FEES THAT FEED ON YOUR FORTUNE

I personally dislike any fees or extra costs that hurt my ability to build equity in my home. Condo association and homeowner's association and maintenance fees eat into your ability to build equity in your home. Any amount of money you must pay that is not directed at the mortgage principal and interest is money that is gone forever, so the key is to minimize all of those extra costs. This is very important. Think of this: If you can afford to pay $65,000 for a condominium that has a $150 per month maintenance fee, you can also afford an $80,000 house. Many people settle for the cheaper home thinking they can't afford the more expensive home. They discount the fact that they are going to pay $150 extra each month for some basic services for the entire community, like cutting the grass and maintaining the community swimming pool if there is one. You could really be living in a bigger home if you wanted and still make money. Look at these numbers: Take the $80,000 mortgage at the same interest rate, 6.3 percent. Your monthly payment for principle and interest would go up from $402 (for a $65,000 loan) to $495. This leaves you with an extra $57 a month and a house worth at least $80,000. Put the $57 into a savings account every month at just 1.5 percent interest and you can look forward to having nearly $23,000 in the bank at the end of thirty years. Or, you could pay the extra $57 a month toward the principle on your home mortgage loan and save over $18,000 in interest while you pay the home off in just over twenty-three years.

There could be many variations on the example given above. It is meant to give you some idea of the incredible wealth-building power of owning your own home. For most people, real estate offers the greatest opportunity to build a richer lifestyle now and a more comfortable financial future. You will live somewhere for the rest of your life so smart real estate investing is a strategy that will serve you for a long time. In fact, real property is one of the best ways to pass wealth on to your family.

Smart ownership of real estate can give you major financial leverage. It can legitimately make anyone a millionaire in a relatively short period of time. It all starts with doing the right things with your primary residence and building from there.

$ $ $ $ $ $ $ $ $ $ $ $ $ $ **10** $ $ $ $ $ $ $ $ $ $ $ $ $ $

It's All about Cash Flow

"For most families, just $100 in extra income each month would make a
major impact on their ability to pay bills on time."

Most people understand the importance of cash flow and are quick to admit the fact that they need more cash coming into their household each month.

For most families, just $100 in extra income each month would have a major impact on their ability to pay their bills on time. In my opinion, managing money is a very, very easy topic to master. Financial professionals tend to make financial matters—just as lawyers tend to do with the law— sound mysterious and difficult. But, the truth is, all you need to know to be successful with your personal finances can be found in this very simple formula: "You need more money coming into your household each month than you have going out for expenses."

I'll bet you agree with that formula and might even be saying to yourself, "No kidding, wise-guy, I knew that already. I didn't need to buy your book to learn what I already knew." Hopefully, you will bear with me and allow me to remind you of some fundamental truths about cash flow and reenergize your understanding of this crucial concept.

It isn't that people don't know they need to increase cash flow beyond their expenses. The need for cash flow is, without question, a well-known concept. But when it comes to actually making it happen, most people fall short of their desires. If the need for cash flow is so well understood, why then, do most families lack the cash flow they need? Why do so many families struggle to pay their bills each month?

MAKING DREAMS COME TRUE

The reason is as simple and fundamental as the formula for success. Most people don't have a solid plan of action. Let me restate that; I think I was a little too easy on you. Most people have *no plan of action at all*. They have dreams. They have what I call the "Someday Syndrome." People say things like, "Someday I won't have to work anymore." Or, "Someday, I'm going to start my own business." They usually say this, by the way, on the way to work. People afflicted with Someday Syndrome are prime candidates for get-rich-quick schemes, because these opportunities usually promise quick, no-effort shortcuts to riches.

The Someday Syndrome is very common. Do you have it? Give yourself this test to find out. Be honest. Have you, in the last thirty to sixty days, said to yourself, or someone close to you, the following: "Someday, I/we are going to _____." Be sure to fill in the blank with whatever it is that you want: Buy a bigger home, pay off credit card bills, get a better job, start a small business, travel around the world, play golf everyday. I think you know the drill.

There is nothing at all wrong with being a dreamer. I am a big dreamer myself. That is what fueled my drive to write this book and do a nationally syndicated radio talk show. But dreams without action to make them happen never have a chance to materialize. Dreaming all the time without seeing your dreams materialize leads to frustration. Frustration often leads to depression and a feeling of powerlessness. Despair is a common feeling that can set in and often can lead to the ruin of families and individual lives.

Unfulfilled dreams, in my opinion, are the leading killer of happiness. Just think of all the things you thought you would accomplish when you were in high school. The world was literally at your disposal when you were seventeen or eighteen years old. You could have had anything or been anyone you wanted. I believe this is true. With few exceptions, especially if you live in the United States of America, you have every opportunity to succeed at what you dream of doing with your life. Somehow, though, most people's lives end up vastly different than what they had imagined.

Dreams without action are not the only roadblock to success. Knowledge without action is also useless. If you doubt this premise, ask yourself why there are professors in colleges and universities across the world who teach successful business practices, yet, how many of them are—or ever become—independently wealthy? In spite of their vast knowledge of the subject of making money, they still go to work each day to earn a living. Teachers have immediate access to all of the known information in the world on creating wealth. For that matter, so do you and I. There are no secrets to becoming wealthy. It has all been written about. There are millions of books about how to generate cash flow. So why do so few of us reach the promised land of independent wealth? Why are the majority of people living paycheck to paycheck?

SEEKING SOURCES OF INCOME

As I have said, one major reason is that people do not run their personal financial lives as they would a business. For some reason, generating income from sources other than their job is foreign to them. Let me ask you this: Are you generating income from a source other than your job? If you are, you are way ahead of more than 90 percent of your fellow consumers. If you are not, you are no different than the majority of people in the world.

Cash flow is the life-blood of business but it is no less important to you and I in our personal lives.

Each day, in e-mails and on the radio show, the most common question I receive sounds something like this: "I am able to make my monthly bill payments, barely, but I don't seem to be getting ahead. What should I do?" My answer often sounds facetious because it is so obvious of an answer. But, it is true, and a very easy thing to do. Increase your cash flow!

What comes to your mind when you think of increasing your income? The answer will give you a good clue as to what your preconceived notions are about generating income. Some of you immediately thought about getting a better job or having to get a part-time job, or, of working overtime at your current place of employment. Others of you thought of investing or starting a small business. Some of you thought about having a garage sale. All of these are possible answers to the question of how you might increase your cash flow. Yes, there were also those of you who immediately thought of buying a lottery ticket. While there certainly are lottery winners, I want to encourage you to think in more realistic terms, and to think of possibilities that have a better chance of occurring than you being struck by lightening. And don't forget to work that lottery ticket purchase into your spending plan!

Now, here is the big, important question: How many of these realistic solutions have you tried this year, or last? Or ever? If you have not attempted to increase your income using any of these techniques, or others not mentioned, you can't really say you have done everything you can do to improve your lifestyle. That would tend to put you into the "dreamer" category. As I said, dreams are good only if they are followed by informed action.

If you are working forty to sixty hours a week and have a family, the idea of working another twenty or thirty hours may be too much for you to consider. And it probably should be. Remember, we are talking about improving your lifestyle. A big part of improving your lifestyle means spending more time at home with your family, not less time. This doesn't mean you have no chance of increasing your income if you don't spend more time at work and less time with your loved ones. It just means you will have to be a bit more creative than the vast majority of your fellow citizens.

Let me take this opportunity to make the point very clearly that you will have to invest time in order to generate additional cash flow. It may not be twenty or thirty hours of overtime a week, or at a part-time job, but you will need to invest some time. It may be time spent preparing for and hosting a yard sale every weekend or time spent researching and starting a small business or investment program. There will be an investment of your time required.

SMART TIME INVESTMENT

Some have called this investment a "smart time investment." You invest time working extra hours at your job. But that investment returns dollars for your hours. No hours of work, no dollars. The smart time investment I am talking about here should yield more of a long-term return on your time investment. You want to find ways to invest your time once and then receive ongoing return-on-investment in the form of cash flow over and over again, even when you stop investing your time.

The idea of investing your time versus spending your time is an important concept that you must understand and adopt if you truly wish to improve your cash flow in a meaningful way. You are investing time. Time is the most precious commodity known to man. None of us know how much time we really have to invest. We all get the same amount of hours in a day, but how many days will we get? Nobody knows. You've no doubt heard the phrase, "Time is money." If you don't have a lot of money, you must invest your time. There is a big difference between spending time and investing time. You spend time watching television if you watch a sitcom. You are investing your time if you watch a television show on investing or starting a small business.

In addition, if you want to start generating income from something other than a job, you will also be required to invest some money as well. It may not be much money, but it will be nearly impossible for you to start any type of legitimate business without some investment of funds. You can't have a yard sale without putting up a sign. Even if the sign is homemade, it will cost something.

The fact that you have to spend some time and money to make some money may be enough to stop you in your tracks. You may be thinking, "I'm in debt and can't even afford to pay my bills. I don't have any money to invest in starting a business." I understand why you would feel that way. However, your only other choice is to stay right where you are now, in the Someday Syndrome. "Someday, I will be out of debt and will be able to start a business, or do something else to generate income, so I won't have to work so hard trading hours for dollars and leave my financial future totally in the hands of my employer."

In the long run, your optimum goal must be to get involved in something that can generate cash flow on an ongoing basis with very little or zero personal labor or hourly time investment on your part. You start by putting in an investment of your time and money in an initial effort. If you have chosen properly, you will not need to work hard for a long time. Your plan should include a time frame for when your endeavor will show positive cash flow. If cash flow is too far down the road, you may want to consider something else before you start. The idea is *not* to get yourself another job—you already have one of those.

When you work at a job, you trade your hours for money. If you don't go to work, you will not generate money. If you start a business or invest properly, your initial efforts can lead to ongoing income even when you are doing things other than your business. At one time, I was involved in the long-distance business. It was just after the long-distance telephone companies were deregulated and many small companies, which were just getting into the long-distance telephone business, needed help marketing their services. I was marketing discounted long-distance service. I loved it.

Once I did the initial work to sign someone up for the new service, every time he made a long-distance call, I would make a small percentage of the monthly bill. Imagine, even when I was sleeping, people I had signed up were making long-distance calls and generating income for my family. This happened twenty-four hours a day, seven days a week.

This same scenario exists in thousands of existing businesses, with new ones popping up every day. Your goal is to get involved in a business or investment that can deliver income around the clock whether you are working the business or not. You may need to hold some yard sales to pay off debt and generate some income to start your real income-generating idea, but that won't go on forever. And don't think you have to reinvent the wheel to be in business. Most successful business people get involved in already existing ventures and improve on them just a bit. I didn't invent long-distance telephone service, but I did come up with some creative ways to get large groups of people interested in cutting their long-distance costs.

YOU DON'T NEED ANOTHER JOB

Many people think that the only way to start a business is to go the traditional route of starting a restaurant or a retail store of some sort. The investment of time and capital to properly do something of that scale is virtually impossible for most working people, so they give up on their dream. In my opinion, your dream really should not be to start a business. Starting a business is a means to an end. The real objective should be to create cash flow from a source independent of your personal labor. One reason I think a large percentage of business start-ups fail is due to the fact that the owners started a new job, not a new business. They did not set up the business to run independently of their personal efforts and so they burn out and things start to slip. You see it all of the time and it is sad to see.

It is actually very easy to rent some space, buy some inventory, print some business cards, and say you are in business. In fact, within twenty-four hours or less, you could set yourself up in business for very little cost right from your kitchen table. According to the Small Business Administration, most small businesses are started with $20,000 or less. But, will you be generating revenue? Probably not. Getting into business is not the goal. If it is, do it today and consider yourself successful. However, the subject of this chapter is cash flow, and without it, your business is doomed. I don't have to tell you that without proper cash flow, your personal financial life is doomed as well.

POSITIVE CASH FLOW

By proper cash flow I mean positive cash flow. No doubt you have heard the term positive cash flow used before. It simply means you actually have money left over at the end of the month. If you end each month with no extra money or are actually in a negative position where you owe more in expenses than you have coming in to cover the bills, you are in a dangerous place and must take action immediately to change things around. You must do whatever it takes legally to get yourself into a positive cash flow position, in business and in your personal life.

I can't tell you how many people I come in contact with who are just a few dollars from positive cash flow. I mean, less than $100 a month short of paying all of their bills in full and on time. That is just $25 a week. Quick, think of five ways to earn $25 a week. I will give you ten seconds. Did you do it? Great, then you just thought of five ways to increase your cash flow by $100 a month.

You may have thought of things like having garage sales, cutting lawns, shoveling snow, setting up a table at the local flea market once a month, typing resumes or college papers, cleaning homes or offices, cooking for others, bringing items to a consignment shop. Some of you thought of your professional or job skills you could offer for sale. If you thought of five ways to create an extra $25 a week and you do all five, you can have $500 a month in extra income. Would $100 or $500 extra each month make a difference in your family's lifestyle? You bet it would. Have you ever seen a neighbor drive by in a brand new car, like a BMW or a Cadillac, and said to yourself, "How can they afford that?" You just answered that question for yourself with the "five ways to $100" exercise.

Sit down and list every skill, interest, and ability you have—or could learn fairly quickly—and you will begin to see how valuable you really are. Then choose the skills that you can translate into cash flow generation without a great deal of time or financial investment. What can you do this week to create some cash flow? What starts out as a way to create $25 a week could eventually grow to a multi-million-dollar business.

PAY ATTENTION TO THE MARKETPLACE

There is lots of advice around about starting businesses. A common piece of advice is to take a hobby or other favorite pursuit and make it into a business. I will admit, there have been cases where people have taken a hobby and grown it into a business. But it really depends on what your hobby is. Is it a hobby that is also enjoyed by millions of other people? If so, then maybe you have a chance of being successful.

I once received some very useful advice from a very successful businessman. We were discussing marketing strategies and how he came up with new products to sell. He told me: "When trying to come up with new things that others would like to buy, never be an audience of one." He went on to explain what he meant by the term, "audience of one." He told me that just because he liked to read the *Wall Street Journal* everyday, he realized more people read tabloids each day. Just because he could afford to shop in the most expensive stores and price had become less important to him, he had to keep in mind that most people live on a fixed income and price really matters to them.

Your personal preferences, while they should play a role in any business decisions you make, must take second place to the desires of the majority of the marketplace you wish to serve; that is, if you want to generate cash flow and profits. There are plenty of companies that are, simply, labors of love for the owner, whether they make money or not. However, these businesses don't necessarily bring their owners closer to positive cash flow.

If the business you create can't run while you are home or on vacation, or doing something else, then it is a job, not a business. If your business is effectively "closed" when you take a day off, you have not separated yourself from having to trade your hours for money.

Since my business is my creativity through my writing, the daily radio show, and other creative endeavors, I could be in the same situation. However, thanks to technology, I can write and broadcast the radio show from just about anywhere on earth. So, to that degree, I have freedom. In my situation, we use leverage to create revenue. My radio show is rebroadcast during the week with some stations airing the show even when I am asleep. Our Web site, *www.mikeshow.com* is open for business twenty four hours a day, and our books and newsletters are available for sale long after I have put in the initial effort to create them.

SMART TAX STRATEGIES

Another great reason to create a small, home-based business is because of the potential tax savings you can create. I am asked constantly for strategies for reducing taxes by people who are working hard at their jobs and hate to see how much money is taken out of their paychecks each payday. One of the first questions I always ask them is if they have a small business. The tax code is friendly to legitimate businesses. Most people dream of being their own boss. By starting a small business, many expenses that were personal now may become partly or fully tax deductible. Business startup and operational expenses, tools, home office furniture, office supplies, cost of goods to be sold, travel, mileage, subscriptions, meals, entertainment and gifts, some insurance premiums, and retirement contributions are some of the many legal business expenses that can help you actually reduce your taxable personal income while you build a small business. IRS Publication 535, "Business Expenses," explains the rules for deducting business expenses very clearly. I suggest you print yourself a copy of this form when you visit *www.irs.gov.*

But remember, the idea is to create cash flow from your business. Your goal is not just to create tax deductions. Most businesses take a few years to see positive cash flow, but when you begin to create positive cash flow, you will create tax liability on your profits. Many state and local governments levy additional taxes upon commercial ventures, and even small, home-based entities are not immune. When you get to the point where your business is creating revenue exceeding your expenses—a surplus—it would make sense to hire a good certified public accountant, tax attorney, or both, to help you structure your business to again minimize your tax liability to the least required by law.

It is important that you understand how to properly utilize the tax deductions that are available to you under the law. As reported in the February 2003 issue of *Kiplinger's Personal Finance Magazine*, 100 million American taxpayers overpaid 2002 taxes by $200 billion. If you are currently overpaying your income taxes, you can actually increase your weekly take-home pay from your job by making a simple adjustment to your W-4 form. Remember, you are the one who tells your employer how much to take out of your paycheck each payday in order to pay your income taxes for you. If you adjust the number of allowances on your W-4 form at work, the amount of money taken out of your paycheck and sent to the government on your behalf would change. The higher the number of allowances you list, the less money taken out of your paycheck. Now, you cannot just take a large number of allowances in order to reduce your tax burden. You are required by law to pay the proper amount of taxes due based on your taxable income. So this strategy is only viable for people who are creating legitimate tax deductions based on IRS guidelines and who itemize their tax returns. If you underpay taxes during the year, you risk audit and fines from the Internal Revenue Service. However, if you overpay, the IRS will give you your money back without interest once you file your annual tax return. Most people overpay their taxes and get a big refund each year about forty-five days after they file their tax return. The average tax refund this year is running $2,400. A simple adjustment in your company's payroll office will give you an instant raise in your take-home pay.

I have heard all of the reasons why people overpay taxes. These excuses include being afraid of being audited by the IRS and liking the idea of getting a big, lump sum of money once a year.

My response to these two very popular reasons for overpaying taxes is the following: One, if you are doing things legally, an audit should not scare you; and, two, that lump sum once a year is coming to you without interest. You would be better off adjusting the number of your personal allowances on your W-4 form, if your situation allows, getting an increase in your take-home pay, and putting the increase into a savings account paying 1 to 2 percent interest. You won't have the government doing the savings work for you anymore but you will be earning interest on your hard-earned money. The extra income might allow you to pay down high interest debt. For example, if you pay off an 18-percent credit card debt with your pay increase, you are effectively earning 18 percent return on that investment. Isn't that better than getting zero percent from Uncle Sam?

What if you could just increase your take-home pay by $25 a week or $100 a month by doing a little tax planning? Yes, it will require you to look at your finances and your taxes this year instead of next April when most people start to deal with their taxes. If you wait until the end of the year to start thinking about your taxes, your opportunity to do anything about how much you owe will be lost. You need cash flow now, so now is the time to plan and make adjustments, which will give you more cash flow.

YOUR CASH FLOW ACTION PLAN

A small home-based business can give you opportunities to lower your tax burden and it can also allow you to create additional income. A small home-based business can lead to something big in your financial future. You could eventually replace your job income totally. It won't happen overnight but you could actually become wealthy with your business or businesses. You are in the right country to make it happen. Wouldn't it be a great story? You start a small business because you needed some extra money to pay off some credit card debts and you end up becoming a millionaire. It happens every day in this great country so don't ever count yourself out of the game.

Whatever you ultimately choose to do, be sure to keep foremost in your mind the fact that you need to create cash flow. You don't want to end up creating even more debt for yourself in an attempt to pay off personal debt by borrowing lots of money to start a business. But, there is nothing wrong with making some short-term investments if there is a high probability of them paying you back within a time frame that is acceptable. If you need quick cash to catch up on some late bills, starting a business that will take twelve months just to break even does not make sense in your situation. It all should start with you taking the time to access your short-term and long-term needs and then creating an action plan that matches your desired outcome.

Short-term goals are things you can accomplish within the next twelve months such as paying off some credit card debt and reducing expenses. Long-term goals help you plan for the next two to five years and might include paying off a car loan, saving a certain amount of money in your child's college fund, and generating enough income from your home-based business to replace the income you now get from your job.

It is very difficult to generate quick cash by starting a business, or through any other investments, because you need some time for any investment to create a return. This fact limits your choices to what is immediately available to you. For most people that means looking for more hours at your job—if you are paid hourly, and more work is available—or, possibly, it means taking on another job. If your short-term goals require quick cash flow, this may be your only option. But, in your long-term plan, the second job should be replaced by something that is a little more family and personal-health friendly.

A very commonly overlooked way to generate additional cash flow each month to help pay your bills is by cutting monthly expenses. I know, this seems such an obvious solution yet, so many of you procrastinate on this very important part of your financial plan. The name of this book is *Spend Your Way to Wealth.* Obviously, we realize spending money is a requirement in life. Where you spend money and how much you spend on everything you buy is the part you can manage successfully. Cutting expenses is not synonymous with cutting your lifestyle. As you must know by now, the popular belief is that cutting expenses requires a great deal of sacrifice and deprivation, but I do not necessarily accept that. I've shown you that if you know how to buy a car correctly, you can still afford to drive your dream car. The same goes for your home, clothing, and every other thing you can think of.

If you want to generate more cash flow, you must start by completing a monthly spending and net-income analysis in order to see where you are spending every penny that is coming into your home. A spending and expense analysis is the only way for you to actually see, in black and white, where you can make some changes in order to free up cash to pay your bills and start to save money. Even if you start to generate more income from a second job or small business, you should complete a spending and income analysis every month, since, as I've stated elsewhere, there is no amount of income that you cannot outspend, if you're not attending to your expenses.

INCREASING CASH FLOW BY LOWERING MONTHLY BILLS AND FEES

When attempting to work on a spending analysis, there seem to be many areas of expenses that are missed. A commonly overlooked area of expense is credit-card interest rates. It is shocking how many people do not know what interest rate they are being charged when they borrow money by using a credit card. Even fewer people know the dollar amount of fees that can be charged on their accounts if they are ever late with a payment or charge more than their limit.

I suggest you call all of your credit-card issuing companies and ask them what your interest rate is on each of your accounts as well as how much they could charge you in fees; also check your annual fee. Next, while you are on the telephone, ask for a lower interest rate. If you have been a good customer and have made on-time payments for the past twelve months, even if you've only made the minimum required payments, chances are good that the creditor will grant your request for a lower interest rate. Competition for customers is fierce right now in the credit card industry. If your company will not lower your interest rate upon your request, and your credit score and credit report are in good shape, I suggest you shop for lower interest rate cards and, if approved, transfer your debt to the new card at the lower interest rate.

While you are on the phone requesting a lower interest rate, be sure to ask the company to eliminate your annual fee if you are paying one. That annual fee represents $25 to $100 that should be in your pocket, not in the credit-card company's coffers. Those companies make enough profit on the interest, late fees, and over-the-limit fees they charge. Again, if the company will not eliminate your annual fee, you may want to shop for a company that does not charge an annual fee. Don't be afraid to ask for these things. You have nothing to lose and cash flow to gain.

Your utility bills offer another overlooked opportunity to cut expenses without cutting into your lifestyle. Turn off lights in unused rooms, shut off the hot water while shaving, and consider canceling your cable television connection for a short while until you can affordably work it into your plan.

Check your long-distance telephone usage and find a cheaper rate. You should not be paying more than 4 or 5¢ a minute for long-distance service. Use e-mail more to communicate with others, or wait for people to call you rather than calling them.

Speaking of telephones, watch out for the costs associated with your cellular telephone. Since so many people have cellular telephones today, they are used without giving thought to the expense. It is very convenient to use a cell phone at the drop of a hat. These costs can really add up if you are not on a monthly plan that matches your level of use. If you are surpassing the amount of included minutes of your plan every month and paying for expensive minutes, talk to your representative about moving to a different plan. If you really take a good look at what you use your cellular telephone for, and were willing to adjust your habits just a little, you could trade a little bit of convenience for a less-expensive monthly cell phone bill. Again, a few more dollars in your pocket at the end of each month is your goal.

Investigate the viability of refinancing your mortgage for a lower interest rate. As I write, mortgage rates are at a forty-year low level and if you are planning to stay in your home for at least the next two or three years, refinancing for a lower interest rate may make sense for you.

Make sure you are not paying outrageous monthly bank fees. This is an area that can quietly eat a big hole in your finances, especially if you use your ATM card a lot at machines that are not owned by your bank. As you read this, someone, somewhere, is taking $10 out of an ATM machine. She will pay a $1.50 fee to the bank that owns the ATM machine for processing the transaction and pay another $1.50 fee to her bank, also for processing the transaction. This represents a grand total of $3, or, a 30 percent fee, to get $10 of her own money out of her bank account. Paying fees like this saps you of cash flow.

Instead of buying your lunch everyday, pack your lunch even if it is for just a month or two. Remember, these are just suggestions. If you enjoy eating out each day, just work it into your monthly spending plan.

There are many ways to create more cash flow in your life and you can start to do many of them today. Life and business both come down to cash flow. That is the system we have. It would be great if we did not need cash to live. We could all go off and pursue the hobbies and other things in life that bring us joy. Until you have enough cash flow separate from your personal labor, you will never be truly free to do what you want when you want.

Approach the task of generating cash flow for your family just as you would if it were for a business you owned or managed. This is the business of you—You, Inc.—and there is no more important business in the world.

11

$ $ $ $ $ $ $ $ $ $ $ $ $ $ $ $ $ $ $ $ $ $ $ $ $ $ $ $ $ $

Internet or InterNOT?

"You may never actually buy anything directly from the Internet. But, you can go shopping armed with reams of information, which makes you a much smarter buyer."

As I write this book, at least 60 percent of Americans have access to the Internet. The number of people signing onto the Internet for the first time is increasing by the hour. The general public's acceptance of the personal computer in the 1980s opened the door for the Internet to become the biggest communication and marketing tool ever in the history of the world so far and for the foreseeable future. Extensive marketing of the World Wide Web has made just about everyone in the world aware of its existence. Even small, remote villages in the most desolate places on earth are getting linked into the Internet.

In spite of all of the incredible exposure the Internet has received during the past several years, I am still often asked, "Does anything exist on the Internet that is worthwhile, or is it all just a bunch of hype?" This question has become more common in the wake of the recent failure of the many dot-com companies. If you are one of those people, like me, who use the

Internet constantly, on a daily basis, you know that there are endless amounts of resources at your disposal on the Web. By the same token, there is also a great deal of clutter—to put it nicely. One reason for there being so much good, and bad, on the Internet is because it is so inexpensive to create a presence by obtaining a domain name, creating some Web pages, and placing those pages, or, uploading them, onto the Internet. Anyone can now have his own personal Web site. Many companies consider having a Web presence to be as necessary as having business cards. You can start a Web page on any subject; in fact, just about every subject is represented on the Internet thousands of times.

BRICK-AND-MORTAR STILL NOT OBSOLETE

In the mid-1990s, as the Internet was just beginning to become popular, I remember the marketing message to business owners very clearly: If you own a business and you are not doing business on the Internet by the year 2000, chances are you will not still be in business. Of course, that turned out to be untrue. But at the time it seemed like it would be a real possibility and businesses flocked to the Internet in order to ensure they would not be outdone by their competition.

As we also now know, many companies thought they could run businesses completely on the Internet without a traditional "brick-and-mortar" presence. With very few exceptions, this has not proven to be viable for most businesses to date. You and I are slow to give up the opportunity to touch and feel a product before we purchase it. For some industries, like travel, the Internet has become a way to make the product more easily available; however, you can still buy a ticket from a travel agent in person if you so desire—that is, if you can find a travel agent who can afford to stay in business. The Internet has given hotels, airlines, and other travel-related companies the ability to cut out the middlemen—the agent—and save lots of money that used to be paid in commissions. We can now do all of the itinerary and pricing research a travel agent used to do from the comfort of our home. We can compare fares on airlines and hotel rooms with the click of a few buttons and buy all of the tickets online.

The Internet shifts a great deal of the workload onto consumers, allowing the travel companies to reduce their staffs and expenses. You would think this savings would go toward lowering costs to consumers and improved quality, wouldn't you? Unfortunately, that has not been the case. In fact, even with the big savings, many airlines are teetering on the brink of bankruptcy.

THE E-EDUCATION OF THE CONSUMER

The bottom line, in my opinion, is that the Internet provides consumers with incredible opportunity to spend their way to wealth by becoming much smarter about the things they buy. The Internet gives us unprecedented access to information about products and the companies that produce and sell them. The real power for consumers is our new ability to comparison shop, not only price, but features and benefits. We can literally shop the world for a better deal on the things we want and need to buy.

You may never actually buy anything directly from the Internet. But you can go shopping at any local store armed with reams of information that you found on the Internet. This will make you a much smarter buyer who is much less likely to get manipulated by salespeople and the sales process and end up feeling ripped off. My wife and I have used the Internet to research vehicle prices before going to the car lot to negotiate. Just in the last six months we have researched clothing, furniture, toys, bedding, computers, sporting goods, and electronic equipment before going to a local retailer to negotiate a purchase. We have always saved money by doing this. In some cases, the retailer was offering a good price and we simply verified that fact.

I've mentioned using the Internet to do research on products and services you are thinking about purchasing. You also can now do quite a bit of information gathering on companies with which you are potentially going to do business. The information available about publicly held companies is staggering. You can find out information about recalls of certain products, lawsuits filed and the outcomes, and complaints about a company and its products. Some places to visit online include the Better Business Bureau (*www.bbbonline.org*), The Federal Trade Commission (*www.ftc.gov*), Yahoo Finance (*www.yahoo.com*), Hoovers Business Information (*www.hoovers.com*), *www.morningstar.com*, Securities and Exchange Commission (*www.sec.gov*), and *www.consumer.gov*, which provides links to consumer information from the federal government.

You can also find out good things about products and companies, often from consumers just like you. There are forums and chat rooms dedicated to discussing certain companies and their products where you can read the comments and experiences of other consumers who have used the product. The Internet can make you a more knowledgeable consumer. What you do with that knowledge is up to you. The best way to find these discussions is to search your topic on the major search engines and by visiting Internet service provider chat rooms that focus on your topic, product, or company.

DISCOUNTS ON THE WEB

We spent an entire chapter of this book discussing the smart use of coupons. You now know how great money-saving coupons are and what a huge impact they can make on your financial future. The Internet makes it even easier to save money and build wealth with coupons. There are thousands of sources of free offers, coupons, and discounts on the Internet. You can literally search for coupons for the items you really want to purchase and then print the coupons right on your printer for free. In fact, coupons will often find you. They will pop up right before your eyes as you visit Web pages. You just need to pay attention. Marketers are throwing money at you electronically and all you have to do is hit the print button or click your mouse. Many people are annoyed by Internet marketing, yet if you walked through the grocery store and people kept popping up in front of your shopping cart waving dollar bills in front of your face to take if you wanted, would you be annoyed? I guess some people would be bothered. But not me. Of course, I am very particular about which advertising I take advantage of, just as I am with the advertising that comes through regular mail, television, radio, and the newspaper. The Internet kind of advertising is just much easier to sift through and delete if you don't want or need the offer.

There are thousands of Web sites specifically dedicated to providing discount offerings. Imagine how cost effective it is for a manufacturer that, up until the Internet's growth and acceptance by consumers, could only reach the public through costly printing of coupons and then paying to deliver them in newspapers and through the mail.

For a company selling products and services, the Internet represents a highly cost-efficient way to reach customers. Companies really want the Internet to succeed and are constantly looking for new ways to attract shoppers and buyers to their Web sites. Can you imagine if companies could do away with the cost of building and running their traditional brick-and-mortar stores? Profits would skyrocket. And so, companies are working hard to find the best ways to attract loyal Internet shoppers. There is a long way to go, but while they are looking for the right strategies, it can only mean good things for all consumers.

Because it is so easy to start a business on the Internet, competition for your eyes, and your spending, is incredibly stiff. One of the best ways to attract visitors to a Web site is to offer discounts, free items, and lots of bargains. Internet marketers use the low-price sales proposition like crazy all over the Internet. You don't see much about quality in these advertisements. At least not yet. It is unfortunate that quality is not a higher priority for these Web merchants, but, the name of the game right now is to create traffic on the Web site. To get people to visit, companies have to offer some compelling reason to the surfer. As each site continues to try to outdo each other, the offers keep getting better.

CUSTOMIZED CUSTOMER SERVICE

The Internet allows companies to customize the offers they present to you when you visit their Web site based on your past behavior and any information you voluntarily provide. For example, if you search for information on a certain brand of a product, the company can capture that information and, when you return to the Web site, offer you a special discount on that brand. Or, if you supply your e-mail address, the company will send you offers designed specifically for your tastes. Unfortunately, most companies are still not using this level of technology to serve customers and entice potential customers. One reason is the cost of the technology. It is relatively expensive for a company to design and develop a sophisticated customer service and marketing system on its Web site. On a positive note, this technology is getting less expensive every day and soon all companies on the Web will utilize some form of it.

You may find my enthusiasm for this marketing technology to be amazing; but remember, I am the guy who loves to receive coupons in my mail. So, of course I am excited to think about receiving money in the form of savings in my e-mail. Imagine two or three clicks of my mouse and I can print out coupons for items I need and want to buy. It is the closest thing I can think of to legally printing money.

Using the Internet, you can shop and save money without leaving your desk. The time savings alone is incredible. I urge you to track the time you save using the Internet and calculate an amount per hour. Think of it as earnings. Use the amount you earn per hour at work as a starting point to calculate your earnings. Think of the time you would have spent in traffic driving to stores, parking, walking around looking for your product and sales help. If you earn $10 an hour at work and you save one hour of driving around town by using the Internet, consider that $10 saved and earned on top of any discounts you found on the Web. You will earn hundreds, if not thousands of dollars a year. Time is money! And that doesn't take into account the money you save by spending the time researching discounts and by simply being a more-informed shopper. Your biggest problem will be what to do with all of the spare time and money you create for yourself.

Another reason for the slow growth of personalized communication between companies and consumers is the public's reluctance to give out too much personal information over the Internet for fear that it will be used to harm them or inundate them with junk e-mail. I understand this. After all, a large part of the Internet's popularity is the ability of surfers to be anonymous. This new technology allows those who want to give some personal information and receive offers to do so while others may remain anonymous if they so choose.

Yet another reason for lack of specialized service from Internet merchants has a great deal to do with prevailing attitudes of merchants about customer service in general. A lack of commitment to customer service in the brick-and-mortar world translates very easily to the Internet. In fact, since the Internet represents such an automated and impersonal way of dealing with customers, I predict a lack of customer service focus will actually flourish on the Internet. As companies find they can make more sales through their Web sites without the cost of so many employees, they will naturally go too far in the direction of automation until customers begin to leave them because of lack of help when it is needed. The Frequently Asked Questions (FAQ) page on many sites can only do so much. Customer service must be a priority for Internet stores because it is a new, intimidating way to buy products for consumers. The consumer experience must be easy and pleasurable. If it appears difficult, or not as enjoyable as shopping at the mall, Internet merchants will suffer a long, cold winter waiting for online shopping to become the preferred shopping method.

BEWARE OF HIDDEN COSTS

When shopping and trying to save money on the Internet, don't forget to factor in the cost of shipping when comparing prices. Often, the cost of shipping, added to the price of the merchandise, can make the difference between a good deal on the Internet and the same price you can get by driving to your local store. Sometimes you might actually end up paying more for an item once shipping and handling is added in. Plus, if the Internet Company is located in your state, and your state has a sales tax, this tax will have to be added to the cost of the item as well.

Free shipping, of course, is the best shipping price. And, many smart Internet merchants are cutting their profit margins on some items and using free shipping as an enticement to sell more products. It is a smart thing to do, especially as they try to establish the Internet as a viable place for consumers to buy most of the things they need everyday.

DISCOUNTS ON DISCONTINUED PRODUCTS

Product-liquidation Web sites are becoming very popular places to save as much as 80 percent on brand name merchandise. To make things even better, these sites are still relatively unknown so it is like shopping in a mall of bargains with just a handful of people shopping with you. Of course, where the Internet is concerned, a handful still means several million shoppers each month. But, relatively speaking, that is a low number of visitors in the world of e-commerce since most people do not buy anything. These e-stores must have millions of visitors going to the sites in order to capture the small percentage of people who actually buy something. Remember, just like any brick-and-mortar store, these Web sites don't make enough money to stay in business unless people are buying merchandise. They might make some money from advertising sales, but the bulk of the income is made through selling products and services. We, as consumers, want these sites to flourish so they can stay in business and continue providing easy access to huge bargains on really good merchandise.

Liquidation sites, because they are selling items at huge discounts, have a lower profit margin built into each sale. Therefore, their return policies may be a bit different than traditional retail Internet sites. It is a good idea before you buy anything—no matter what type of Web site you are shopping at—to acquaint yourself with the return policy. Some sites offer very liberal return policies, give unlimited time to return an item, and will refund you the full amount of the expenditure. Other sites have much stricter guidelines about returning items and limit both the time you have to return an item and the amount you may receive as a refund. Some sites also may charge a restocking fee if you send something back. Really good sites will offer buyers a price protection policy: If you find a lower price on the same product within a certain time frame, they will refund the full amount of the difference or more. Knowing the rules of any store you choose to do business with will always save you a lot of stress if the product does not turn out to fit your needs. Overstock.com is one of many popular liquidation sites.

THE VIRTUAL CATALOG

Internet shopping is not much different than shopping through catalogs. Catalog shopping, which is more than a hundred years old, is certainly a much slower process. It is also much more expensive for the merchant to use catalog marketing, which naturally increases the cost of merchandise to the consumer. And, unless you receive thousands of catalogs each month in the mail, your selection of products is very limited. But, the basic premise of providing an efficient shopping experience for the consumer is the same in both mediums. Both offer unique advantages to the seller of goods and the buyer. The Internet can provide shoppers with a much more interactive sales presentation of any product. You can actually get involved in the design of your own products online. Car manufacturers were one of the first to use this technology allowing you to actually choose colors, body types, and features of a car and see the finished product in a 360-degree view so you can make changes. Some clothing manufacturers offer sites where you can create a computer image of yourself with your measurements. You can virtually see yourself wearing the clothes you are thinking of buying.

Catalogs are much less flexible with product presentation. With only one or two static photographs of the item and a list of colors and sizes to choose from it is a much less informed buying decision. It really is the way things were done in, "the old days," but still a viable and lucrative business until consumers totally embrace the Internet and all of its advantages.

The one advantage that catalogs have over Web sites is the fact that a catalog can be mailed directly to your home while Web sites have to spend a lot of money to entice people to visit. It takes more work on the consumer's part to go to a Web site than it does to take a catalog out of the mailbox. The catalog is right in your face. This is a huge advantage in addition to the fact that consumers are very used to buying from catalogs. Just about all companies who use catalogs have added Web sites. These companies realize the benefits of technology and will slowly phase out use of the catalogs. In the meantime, as they fight with the Internet for your precious dollars, you can demand top quality for the best possible price, or you can shop elsewhere. You have unlimited choices.

A WORD ABOUT SECURITY

Security also is a very important issue that Internet merchants must deal with. I would like to give you a few words of caution, especially if you are new to the online world. The Internet has provided a new frontier for every brand of con artist and thief you can imagine. The crime of identity theft is flourishing, in part due to the incredible ease with which computer networks and personal information can be stolen or "hacked." Security on the Internet has improved by necessity over the years and technology such as encryption—which codifies data, making it more difficult to decipher and read—has helped to keep the "techno-thieves" off balance. You should not be scared away, though. I believe that you still stand a greater risk of having someone steal personal information from your mailbox than you do of someone stealing your information from a secure database. But, even Microsoft's computers have been broken into by hackers, proving the highest levels of security are not foolproof.

Internet merchants have a great deal of responsibility to keep your personal information as safe as possible when you trust them with it. However, you have an even bigger responsibility to protect yourself from cyber criminals. As I mentioned, the Internet has opened the doors to criminals who hide behind computer screens when they steal. These criminals can use your personal information to obtain credit cards, car loans, and even mortgages in your name.

To protect yourself online and offline, follow these simple steps:

➤ Don't give out personal information including your social security number, date of birth, bank account numbers, credit card numbers, and driver's license numbers unless you completely trust the person, company, or site requesting the information. Never give personal information online unless you are assured your information is being entered into a secure database. Never e-mail your personal information unless your information is being encrypted before being sent through the Web. Since information sent on the Internet is electronic, like a cell phone call, it can be intercepted. The key is to be very careful with what you transmit.

➤ Be especially careful with e-mail solicitations sent to you by complete strangers. If anyone e-mails you asking you to send personal information your radar should go up immediately. No governmental agency or law enforcement agency will e-mail you, unannounced, asking for personal information. Be careful if you are sent an e-mail telling you that you are the winner of a drawing or a sweepstakes. You may be asked to submit your personal information in order to process your winnings. Any consumer scam that has been tried over the telephone or through the mail has shown up on the Internet. Just don't let greed get the best of you and don't let anyone talk you into doing something impulsively before you can check everything out to make sure the offer and the company are legitimate. The Federal Trade Commission, at *www.ftc.gov*, keeps track of these Internet-related scams and it is a good idea to visit the Web site once in a while to keep aware of the latest problems. There is also a great deal of information about keeping safe from theft, both online and offline. The FTC covers a wide variety of consumer topics on its Web site and provides consumers with a good understanding of the protections that exist for you, even providing official complaint forms online. It is user-friendly and one of the best government sites I have ever visited. I visit the site often and suggest you do the same.

It is a good idea to order copies of your credit report from the three credit reporting agencies, Equifax, Experian, and TransUnion, at least once a year. You can do this online since all of these companies have Web sites. If you use your credit cards a lot, whether on the Internet or offline, you are probably best served by checking your credit reports twice a year. There are several credit report monitoring programs available now that will alert you anytime unusual use patterns seem to be occurring with your credit cards. For example, if you normally don't spend large amounts with your card and one day several thousand dollars is charged to the card, you might get an alert from this monitoring company to make sure the expense is authorized. Many credit card companies will offer this service without cost as a matter of their own internal security, so be sure to ask the companies that handle your accounts if they offer such service before you invest in any outside monitoring program.

WWW: THE DOORWAY TO ENDLESS POSSIBILITIES

The efficiencies provided by the Internet are endless. You can lower your long-distance telephone rates, check your bank account, change the address on your driver's license in most states, and order dinner to be delivered, all in a few minutes, from the comfort of your home. You can chat with people all over the world, research any fact, and order any book ever published. You can work from home thanks to the Internet. You can complete and file your taxes online. In your spare time you can start a small business and help your fifth-grader complete a report for school that would put the encyclopedia-researched, hand-copied fifth grade reports of my generation to shame. The Internet is now accessible through a hand-held computer called a Personal Digital Assistant (PDA), and your cellular telephone. I imagine, eventually, watches and other pieces of small jewelry will have computer chips inside of them, which will give us even more efficient access to the Internet.

One of the most exciting uses of the Internet is online education. It is called e-learning. You can take courses on any subject you choose as long as you have access to a computer and can log onto the Internet. All levels of college degrees are offered through the Internet. You can attend, remotely, some of the most prestigious colleges and universities in the world and earn a degree online. The great part is, most online study allows you to attend class and study twenty-four hours a day. You can "go to class" on the Internet when it is convenient for you. This will allow many more people, who cannot attend traditional college classes, to improve their knowledge and expertise. We will become a smarter world, and, I think, a more peaceful world as the education level increases globally.

Easier access to higher education will make it possible for people to boost their income. This is really an exciting by-product of the Internet. We will become wealthier people as a result of having easier access to more education and training.

You can still live a very happy, fulfilling life without ever touching a computer and logging onto the Internet, but it is getting harder and harder to stay out of the way of e-commerce, especially as state and local governments begin to embrace the technology and realize it is a much cheaper and more efficient way to deliver information and services to citizens.

With so many good things available from the Internet, even though there are some security issues to be concerned with, when I am asked, Internet or InterNot, my suggestion is, Internet—absolutely!

12

Live a Richer Lifestyle Starting Today

"The rewards for those who persevere far exceed the pain that must precede the victory."
—Ted Engstrom and R. Alec Mackenzie

If you asked people to define their idea of a richer lifestyle, it would be defined in a million different ways by a million different people. To some people it means having more money with which to buy material things. To others, it means having more things of higher quality or an improved social status. To many, a richer lifestyle simply means more time to spend with family and less time spent working to make money. A richer lifestyle may be just a few credit card payments away for you. If you are living under the burden of a huge debt load, you may feel richer once you get the debt paid down to a manageable size. For most, a richer lifestyle would be a life free from the worry and stress of struggling to pay the bills. Others might define a richer lifestyle as one full of creative or charitable pursuits. And, for some, a richer lifestyle means nothing less than living the life of a multi-millionaire.

ARE YOU WILLING TO DO THE WORK?

In whatever way you envision a richer lifestyle, the key thing to know is that you can have that lifestyle virtually right away. No, you won't be a multi-millionaire overnight. But you can greatly improve your enjoyment of life starting today. If anything, my message is take responsibility for improving your financial life. There really is no magic to it. As you have read, it takes some work. In a lot of cases, it will be hard work because most of you have never gone to the trouble of stretching beyond your comfort zone in order to get the things you really want in life. The world is full of plenty of examples of people who overcame incredible hardship and disadvantage to build wonderful, fulfilling, and what many would call rich, lives. These people did not luck into success. They earned it. They worked for it. Somewhere along the line, they learned the important lesson that I have tried to impart to you in this book. Setting clear financial goals, taking action, and persevering through the difficult times will get you where you want to go.

We are lucky enough to be living in the greatest country in the world where financial opportunity surrounds us. People come to the United States from everywhere in the world to participate in our system. It is easy for us to take our good fortune for granted and become complacent. There are people around you that would try to convince you that someone owes you a free lunch; perhaps that our government should take care of us. You and I know that this thinking couldn't be further from the truth. However, you may feel victimized by the financial system or your current financial status. It is easy to blame the system for being unfair. You may blame fate or others for your financial problems.

Our current economic environment doesn't make positive thinking any easier: High levels of unemployment, record personal bankruptcies, high consumer debt, corporate scandal on Wall Street, and an uncertain economic outlook for the near future. No matter how bleak things may seem, there is still opportunity for you to financially do better tomorrow than you are doing today. You can act to take advantage of any economic environment. You have taken a large step in reading this book and, hopefully, you will read many others on the subject of financial improvement. While others wallow in self-pity and blame the system for their situation, you have begun to do the right things that will get you where you want to go.

FOR BETTER OR WORSE, MONEY MAKES THE WORLD GO 'ROUND

As I have often said, there is very little in life that does not have to do with money. Try to think of something, somewhere, in your life that does not, somehow, rely on money or is affected by money in some way. The most benevolent of charitable organizations must have money to stay in business. Money makes the world go 'round. You've no doubt heard that saying before. That is the system we are in. We don't have to love money or the idea that we need it, but we can accept the system we have, realizing there is no way to avoid the need for money to support our lives. Once you decide to accept the rules of the game, and to play the game to win for yourself and your family, then you will have a distinct advantage. Choosing not to play the money game means you automatically lose because too many other people have already chosen to play. Try telling your credit card company, your utility company, the car dealer, or your landlord that you refuse to play the money game.

Our system requires that you utilize the monetary system to buy and sell things that allow you to survive. It is up to you to decide whether your experience is going to be enjoyable or miserable. I believe you can be happy no matter where you are financially. But, I also believe that everyone would like to do better than they are doing right now. No matter how rich or how poor, everyone would like to step up a notch in lifestyle. It may be a subtle improvement, but an improvement just the same. If you lose the drive to do better financially, I believe you will do worse. There is no standing still when it comes to money. I've said it before and I'll repeat myself because this is an important point: Either you are making money or you are spending money.

Most are spending more than they are earning and that is causing them to live a lifestyle that is below what they truly desire. If that describes your situation, it is your time to change things around. It is your time to gain the advantage over those who have financially taken advantage of you. Use the lessons of this book. Seek out more knowledge everywhere it is available. Determine to do better and slowly you will begin to enjoy the changes that will come only as a result of your hard work and focus on succeeding.

YOUR ROADMAP TO A RICHER LIFE

You have to start by envisioning your richer lifestyle. Clearly see yourself in the financial situation you have only dreamed of up until now. That vision will be your spark. It will give you the beginnings of your road map toward a richer lifestyle. It is different than a dream. Everyone dreams. There is no action associated with dreams. A dream is like a wish. You can dream a great deal but never do anything to make the dream come true. Consciously envisioning yourself and your family enjoying the kind of lifestyle that will make you happy is the first step toward discovering what it will take to make it happen.

Step two is to decide precisely what you will have to do next to begin to move toward making that lifestyle a reality. We have discussed many of the things that can help start you on your way in this book. It is a fairly simple process to take stock of where you are now and what you have to do to get where you want to go. They say that most people spend more time planning a vacation than they do planning their financial future. Ironically, if you just take the time to properly plan your financial future, you can take many more vacations to much better locations.

By just completing your spending plan, I contend that your lifestyle will improve to a great extent. The spending plan will at least give you some real control over whatever amount of money you are dealing with in your life. It may not be millions of dollars that you are working with, but you will know how it is being used and you will be in a position to manipulate your use of your money so that you can improve your lifestyle. By reallocating some money toward paying down high interest debt more quickly, you will generate a higher rate of return than you previously were getting by only making minimum payments. In fact, only making minimum payments was costing you money as the interest on your debt compounded.

By becoming a smarter shopper, a Power Buyer, you will definitely improve your lifestyle. There is no question that increasing your buying power by 10 percent, 20 percent, or more, puts tax-free income right onto your family's bottom line. I like to think conservatively at first. What if you could just keep an extra $25 a week in your account? That $100 a month is often the difference between making a mortgage or car payment, and foreclosure or repossession. It could be the difference between new toys for your kids on birthdays and holidays or, perhaps, no gifts at all. It is for reasons like these that I get so excited about the power of making the smallest changes in the way you are managing your income and expenses. Small changes can have an enormous, sometimes life-changing, effect.

A great deal of change happens when your attitude about money changes. When you feel in control, you take on a new persona when it comes to your finances. It is a confident persona. You feel more comfortable dealing with money issues and decisions. You are no longer intimidated when it comes to doing things within the financial system. You realize you are the buyer of financial services and should be treated as such. You will no longer be intimidated when you walk onto a car dealer's lot or into the mortgage broker's office. You can talk to loan officers and other financial professionals without the fear that they know more about your money than you. Your family and those close to you will notice your new-found confidence and it will help them. You will become a better role model for your children when it comes to handling money. You will be a more productive employee or a more successful businessperson when you get a handle on your finances. Successful attitudes are contagious.

Financial problems or concerns are closely linked to a whole host of physical ailments, from stress-related sleeplessness and anxiety to more serious mental breakdowns, heart attacks, and stroke. If a richer lifestyle in your vision includes better health, seizing control of your finances can bring incredible health benefits.

If you want to supercharge your quest for a richer lifestyle, once you get a handle on your financial situation and can begin to be generous, start to give money to good, charitable causes. Help people by spending some of your money. There are financial benefits to be had when you give to charities but, in addition, this act will bring a much richer feeling to your life beyond anything you can imagine financially. It truly is better to give than to receive; it is spiritual and it is moral, and I believe the good deeds you do will come back to you and your loved ones many times over.

I have had the rare opportunity during the past several years to help many families who were in financial need. Through my work, I hope I have made some of those lives richer.

This book was a labor of love for me. This final chapter of the book marks the ending to a project that has been a major part of my life and those around me. It also marks a great beginning, as it will hopefully inspire you and thousands of people like you to reach for your financial goals. I look forward to the opportunity of sharing my message with the world and I hope you will help me. Now that you are more aware of the many ways in which we keep ourselves from building wealth, I hope you will reach out to those around you and try to help them. It is through a growing community of smart Power Buyers that our impact as consumers will truly be felt in the marketplace.

Thank you for reading my book and congratulations on your decision to spend your way to wealth.

ABOUT THE AUTHOR

Mike Schiano, "The Debt Buster," is a native of Providence, Rhode Island, and grew up in South Florida where he graduated from North Miami High. He received a Bachelors degree in Political Science from the University of Central Florida in Orlando, Florida, and earned the prestigious Certified Professional Manager designation in 2000. He is also a Certified Credit Counselor.

Mike's philosophy is being smart about spending and managing money, whether it's for mortgages, savings, taxes, kids, food, college, or retirement.

Since 1992, he has been involved in bringing personal financial education to families across America through his work with various companies. He has worked closely with some of America's preeminent self-help experts and he joined the non-profit organization InCharge Institute of America in 1998. He currently is president of Be InCharge, Inc., a company created to help consumers make more money, save more money, and make smarter financial decisions. To meet that goal, Mike helped develop the Be InCharge Club, America's Financial Fitness Center (*www.beinchargeclub.com*).

Mike hosts the nationally syndicated radio talk show *The Mike Schiano Show*, as well as *A Minute with Mike*. Both of these popular programs focus on consumer and financial advice. He enjoys making money matters understandable for real people with real problems.

Mike's career in radio began in 1981 and eventually led to work in television, film, and public speaking. He also has been writing about personal finance for the past ten years and currently hosts "Ask the Debt Buster" for Profina Debt Solutions Web site, where he receives and answers thousands of questions each year from people facing difficult financial situations. In addition, he hosts his own informational Web site, *www.mikeshow.com* and publishes the weekly e-zine, *The DebtBuster*.

An entrepreneur, avid athlete, and musician, he lives in Orlando, Florida, with his wife Lori and their three children.

Index

BOOKS FROM ALLWORTH PRESS

Feng Shui and Money: A Nine-Week Program for Creating Wealth Using Ancient Principles and Techniques
by Eric Shaffert (paperback, 6 × 9, 256 pages, $16.95)

The Money Mentor: A Tale of Finding Financial Freedom
by Tad Crawford (paperback, 6 × 9, 272 pages, $14.95)

Your Will and Estate Plan
by Harvey J. Platt (paperback, 6 × 9, 224 pages, $16.95)

Your Living Trust and Estate Plan: How to Maximize Your Family's Assets and Protect Your Loved Ones, Third Edition
by Harvey J. Platt (paperback, 6 × 9, 336 pages, $16.95)

Estate Planning and Administration: How to Maximize Assets and Protect Loved Ones
by Edmund T. Fleming (paperback, 6 × 9, 272 pages, $14.95)

What Money Really Means
by Thomas M. Kostigen (paperback, 6 × 9, 240 pages, $19.95)

Legal Forms for Everyone, Fourth Edition
by Carl W. Battle (paperback, 8 $\frac{1}{2}$ × 11, 224 pages, includes CD-ROM, $24.95)

Winning the Divorce War: How to Protect Your Best Interests
by Ronald Sharp (paperback, 5 $\frac{1}{2}$ × 8 $\frac{1}{2}$, 192 pages, $14.95)

Turn Your Idea or Invention into Millions
by Don Kracke (paperback, 6 × 9, 224 pages, $14.95

The Entrepreneurial Age: Awakening The Spirit of Enterprise in People,Companies, and Countries
by Larry C. Farrell (hardcover, 352 pages, 6 $\frac{1}{2}$ × 9 $\frac{1}{2}$, $24.95)

Old Money: The Mythology of Wealth in America
by Nelson W. Aldrich, Jr. (paperback, 6 × 9, 340 pages, $16.95)

The Secret Life of Money: How Money Can Be Food for the Soul
by Tad Crawford (paperback, 5 $\frac{1}{2}$ × 8 $\frac{1}{2}$, 304 pages, $14.95)

The Money Mirror: How Money Reflects Women's Dreams, Fears, and Desires
by Annette Lieberman and Vicki Lindner (paperback, 6 × 9, 232 pages, $14.95)

Please write to request our free catalog. To order by credit card, call 1-800-491-2808 or send a check or money order to Allworth Press, 10 East 23rd Street, Suite 510, New York, NY 10010. Include $5 for shipping and handling for the first book ordered and $1 for each additional book. Ten dollars plus $1 for each additional book if ordering from Canada. New York State residents must add sales tax.

To see our complete catalog on the World Wide Web, or to order online, you can find us at *www.allworth.com.*